SURRENDER

SECURE GOD'S BEST FOR YOUR LIFE

WAYNE SCHMIDT

wesleyan
PUBLISHING HOUSE
wphstore.com
Indianapolis, Indiana

Copyright © 2017 by Wayne Schmidt
Published by Wesleyan Publishing House
Indianapolis, Indiana 46250
Printed in the United States of America
ISBN: 978-1-63257-122-9
ISBN (e-book): 978-1-63257-099-4

Schmidt, Wayne, 1957- author.
Surrender : secure God's best for your life / Wayne Schmidt.
Indianapolis : Wesleyan Publishing House, 2017. | Includes
    bibliographical references.
LCCN 2017003608 (print) | LCCN 2017005380 (ebook) | ISBN
    9781632571229 (pbk.) | ISBN 9781632570994 (e-book)
LCSH: Submissiveness--Religious aspects--Christianity.
LCC BV4647.A25 S36 2017 (print) | LCC BV4647.A25 (ebook) |
    DDC 248.4--dc23
LC record available at https://lccn.loc.gov/2017003608

To Jan Christoffersen Schmidt, who has walked beside me in nearly every offering plate moment of my life.

To my parents—my dad, Wayne (1932–1993), my mom, Jackie, and stepdad, Delos Tanner—for modeling submission to God as the best way to live for what matters and lasts.

To those who God used to speak into my life in the offering plate moments—Dick Wynn, Kevin Myers, Paul Anthes, Jerry DeRuiter, Kyle Ray, and other beloved brothers and sisters in Christ.

To my Lord and Savior Jesus Christ, who lived a life of "nevertheless, not my will, but yours be done" in full obedience to the Father, even to death on the cross.

And with grateful acknowledgement to Lawrence Wilson, who stretched me to write to my full potential and helped me take this book to a level of greater impact.

Contents

Preface

MOST OF US WOULD RATHER STAND OUR GROUND OR PERHAPS AVOID THE CONFLICT ALTOGETHER.

It takes a bit of courage to pick up a book titled *Surrender*. For most people, the call to surrender triggers a fight-or-flight response. If your first response to a challenge, even from God, is to acquiesce, that is exceedingly rare. Most of us would rather stand our ground or perhaps avoid the conflict altogether. The very idea of surrender is distasteful at best, although it seems like the only response we can make in some situations. What else can you do when you're afraid or overwhelmed or exhausted? Surrender is a last resort, a desperation move.

My aim in writing this book is to change your mind about the meaning of surrender so you will be willing to offer yourself ever more fully to Christ. It is only by responding with faith to those challenging, sometimes painful, moments when Jesus beckons us to follow him in deeper surrender that we can be transformed and change dramatically. Only then will our lives be transformed into his likeness. Resist God's call to surrender, and you will remain as you are. Join Jesus in saying to the Father, "Not my will, but yours be done," and you will experience transformation. Sanctification comes when you are willing to offer your entire life as a gift to God.

That's a lesson I've learned over many years of spiritual conflict, resistance, and by finally surrendering myself to God's will time and time again. Over the nearly fifty years since my first moment of surrender, I have seen that pattern played out many times. Each time has led to a deeper level of commitment to Christ and an increased level of fruitfulness in ministry. I share my experiences and reflections in the sincere hope that they may prompt you to surrender yourself more fully to God and experience the transformed life as a result.

To that end, I have organized this book not in two sections, but into two kinds of chapters. The first are those that describe my experiences, which I label *offering plate moments* (more on that a bit later). These chapters are like a peek inside my daily journal. In them I'm candid about my most significant spiritual challenges. I talk about my inner conflict, the fears, emotions I experienced, the reasons I initially resisted God's call, and my eventual surrender to his will. You may see a bit of yourself in these chapters, for our experience as human beings and as disciples of Jesus no doubt have a lot in common. We're all weak, perhaps in different ways.

Over the years I have learned that my spiritual experiences are only half of the story. I have discovered that a moment of surrender may be short-lived unless supported and extended with understanding. The practice of theological reflection—examining a situation through the lenses of Scripture, the traditions of the church, our own experiences, and reason—helps us put words, resolves, spiritual principles, and, ultimately, actions around our spiritual breakthroughs. So the second type of chapter in this book describes my reflections on moments of spiritual surrender. These chapters draw biblical principles, helpful practices, and other lessons gleaned from my experience. From these chapters I hope you will gain understanding about the dynamics of spiritual surrender that will support you in following through on the commitments you make. These reflection chapters draw heavily from Romans 12, a classic text on the concept of sanctification and one that has been foundational in my thinking.

Experience and reflection: those are the two halves of this book, and the chapters on experience and reason alternate throughout. One chapter describes a challenge I faced, and the next examines the biblical and theological principles that underlie it. If you read only the experience chapters, which you are most welcome to do, you'll find something of a spiritual memoir. If you read only the reflection chapters, you'll find a book of scriptural principles and helpful insights. As a whole, I hope the work offers both the inspiration and the understanding that will enable you to respond to God's call to surrender in your life with a resounding "Yes!"

God's Best vs. Your Best

....

**THE DECISION TO
SURRENDER SET
THE COURSE FOR
THE REST OF
MY LIFE.**

My first semester at college
was anything but peaceful.
The preceding spring had been
one of the most contentious
seasons in recent history. It
seemed that half of the world
was bent on forcing the other
half into submission. John
Mitchell, H. R. Haldeman,
and John Ehrlichman, aides
to former President Richard
Nixon, were found guilty of
conspiracy in the Watergate
affair and surrendered
themselves to federal prison.
World chess champion Bobby

Fischer engaged in a fierce battle with the World Chess Federation over match rules, eventually refusing to defend his title against Russian Garry Kasparov. Fischer was forced to surrender his crown. Domestic terrorists bombed the U.S. State Department's office in Washington, D.C., in an attempt to bring the U.S. government to its knees. Not surprisingly, the government refused to surrender. And the decades-long war in Vietnam finally ended as South Vietnam unconditionally surrendered to North Vietnam following the fall of Saigon.

Most of those conflicts had little to do with me, and I happily entered Grand Rapids Junior College that fall to major in business. Yet, as the autumn leaves began to fall, I found myself embroiled in an intense conflict of my own, one that could end only in an unconditional surrender. Though I didn't realize it at the time, this battle—and the white flag that I finally waved over my young heart—would set the spiritual pattern for my entire life. It was then, as a eighteen-year-old eagerly considering the prospect of graduation, independence, and the many life choices that would follow, that I discovered the unparalleled value of the very thing that co-conspirators, chess champions, and statesmen alike were bent on avoiding. I learned the power of surrender.

My conflict may sound benign to some, but I assure you that it produced a deep spiritual divide within my heart and threatened to derail my growing relationship with God. You see, I felt called to enter the ministry, and, like Jonah, I didn't want to go. Throughout my teen years, I had sensed a call to ministry, but two complicating factors raised enough doubt to reinforce my natural resistance to the idea. This became the ammunition I used in my battle of the wills with God.

The first complication sprang from the wonderful relationship I had with my good Dutch grandmother, Cecil Cole. Grandma Cole was a formative force in our entire family and in my own life. She had concluded that I would make a good pastor, and she pronounced it so. Looking back on those days and remembering my grandmother's maturity and wisdom, I recognize that she simply had the insight to see in me what I could not yet see in myself. She was right about my call to ministry, but I had not yet discerned that call. I was determined that *if* I were to enter the ministry, it would be because God, not my grandmother, had called me.

My hesitation was not unfounded. Even then I knew of too many peers who felt trapped in the ministry after being goaded there by family expectations. During the mid-1970s, this catch phrase was commonly used in personal evangelism: "God loves you and has a wonderful plan for your life." I believed that was true, yet my call to ministry had begun to sound more like "God loves you, and Grandma has a wonderful plan for your life." I knew I had to make this choice independent of others' expectations, and that set up a resistance to God's call within my heart.

The second complication was what I call my wiring, the particular combination of temperament, abilities, intellect, and emotions that make me who I am. Many wonderful shepherds had served my home church during my youth. They were godly pastors, yet I perceived them to be very different from me in temperament and gifting. They excelled in pastoral care, counseling, and preaching—strengths I admired but didn't possess. During high school, I had worked for my dad in the construction business. While I respected our pastors, Dad was my hero. I deeply admired the integrity with which he conducted the business as well as his contribution to our church as a lay leader. I envisioned following in his footsteps and building our family business into a real estate development company. I concluded that my entrepreneurial bent positioned me to be a businessperson, not a pastor. "I'm just not cut out for ministry," I thought. After high school graduation, I entered a local college as a business major and kept working in the construction business. I had no intention of surrendering my future to enter the ministry.

Around October, two circumstances coincided with my hesitancy over ministry to form a perfect storm of doubt and confusion. First, while walking through the school library, I happened to notice a book that questioned the reality of Christ's resurrection. I wasn't taking any religion courses, and I have no idea how that book came to my attention. Likely, it was the work of the Enemy. I read the book and my eyes were opened, so I thought, to a new way of thinking about the faith I had treasured just weeks earlier. I had discovered doubt. The second circumstance was an illness. Like so many other college freshmen, I contracted mononucleosis. Though I kept attending classes, I suffered extreme fatigue, sore throat, head and body aches—all the classic symptoms. I was weak, exhausted, filled with doubts about my faith and dread about the prospect of entering ministry. I lay on the couch, pulled a pillow over my head, and tried desperately to shut out the voice of God.

It didn't work. My sense of God's leading grew so compelling that I realized I would have to answer that call, or my refusal would shut down my heart, withering my relationship with God. Not only my career, but also my very soul, was at stake.

By early December, I had reached a point of desperation. Not knowing quite what to do, I reached out to a friend and mentor named Dick Wynn. Dick was the leader of Youth for Christ in west Michigan and was a true kingdom entrepreneur. I admired his innovative approaches to reaching people for Christ and his bold faith that produced a burning desire to make a difference in the lives of young people in Michigan and around the world. Still in his thirties, Dick had already made multiple overseas trips to share the gospel. He would eventually visit seventy-five nations, literally circling the globe twenty-five times. I trusted Dick because of his authentic faith and willingness to think outside the box, something few church leaders seemed willing to do in those days. He was also an ordained minister in The Wesleyan Church, my own denomination. I had a sense that if anyone could help me resolve this question, it would be Dick. He agreed to meet with me to talk about my call to ministry. I had decided to keep my deeper doubts to myself.

We met in Dick's office on Kalamazoo Avenue, a basement space donated to Youth for Christ by a local physician. I was ill at ease, but Dick's round face and ready smile made it easy to open up about my struggle. My first tack was to suggest that I could do more for the kingdom as a businessman than as a pastor. I was already a volunteer with Youth for Christ. I suggested that I could go into the real estate development business and continue donating time and money to support the cause, something I knew would appeal to Dick. However, he would have none of it.

"That won't solve your spiritual problem," Dick said plainly. "You can't substitute your own plans for God's will. You need to get to the bottom of this now, or you'll never find peace."

I changed course and pitched my line about being called by Grandma, not God.

"I get it," Dick said, "but you're thinking wrong." I was eager to hear more. "In the first place, your grandmother just may be right. If God has called you, wouldn't she be able to see it?"

"But what about this conflict I'm feeling?" I asked.

"Let me ask you this," Dick said. "If you are *not* called to ministry, why would there be any struggle?"

It was a fair point. It was beginning to appear that I was fighting against God and not Grandma after all.

Dick went on. "Are you sure you'd have to become something you're not in order to be a pastor? Isn't it possible that God can use your 'wiring' for his purpose?"

That made sense too. After all, God was clearly using Dick's boundless energy and innovative ideas for the kingdom. Why not my entrepreneurial drive? God would later make many changes in my personal character and relational capacity, but that conversation helped me understand that if God himself had given me these particular strengths, then he could certainly sanctify them for his purpose.

I was feeling better already, but Dick wasn't finished with me yet. After a long pause in the conversation, he leveled his gaze at me. "Wayne, the real question you're facing has nothing to do with a call to ministry."

Really? It sure felt as if it did.

Dick pressed the point home. "Do you believe that surrendering yourself to God is really the best thing you can do? Or do you think God's will for your life is somehow second best?"

For me, that question was the answer. I'd been resisting God as if he were meddling in my plan for a happy life. My mind had even recruited doubts about the resurrection in the service of my obstinate will. In fact, God's will for us is always higher, better, and more satisfying than the dreams we have for ourselves.

I came away from my meeting with Dick feeling a great sense of relief. Our conversation opened a release valve on the spiritual pressure that had been building within me for months—even years. That evening was critical in helping me to hear God's voice more clearly. It also helped to break down my resistance to following God's call. Within a few weeks, I moved fully from resistance to surrender. When my pastor, Doyle Brannon, heard that I'd embraced a call to ministry, he wasted no time. A few weeks later, he graciously drove me the two hundred and fifty miles to Marion College, now Indiana Wesleyan University, where I enrolled in ministerial studies. I would begin classes there the next fall. That decision to surrender set the course for the rest of my life, and not just professionally. It became a pattern for spiritual conflict leading to discernment and finally trust that would play out over and over again as I continued to learn the lesson of surrender.

A New Definition of Surrender

....

THIS IS YOUR TRUE AND PROPER WORSHIP.

ROMANS 12:1

The root of my struggle as an eighteen-year-old was my wrong understanding of the concept of surrender. As with most people, the very word *surrender* left a bad taste in my mouth. I understood it to be synonymous with quitting, failure, or submission to another's domination. So I wanted nothing to do with it. My conversation with Dick Wynn helped me understand surrender in a new and more accurate way. That understanding was critical in motivating me to surrender my entire life to God, including my vocational plans. Contrary to popular thought, surrender to God is not an occasion for shame, regret, or defeat. It is precisely the opposite. It is a spiritual victory that produces a deep sense of peace and sets the stage for future fruitfulness. In the spiritual life, surrender leads to victory. In fact, there can be no spiritual progress without it.

The Struggle behind the Struggle

As momentous as my 1975 surrender was in shaping the trajectory of my life, the real work of God at that stage of my life was something far deeper than a career choice. God was not simply calling me to enter pastoral ministry; he was calling me to the complete surrender of myself that would result in the Holy Spirit permeating every dimension of my life. That was the struggle behind the struggle. To accept the call to ministry, I had to realize that surrendering my will to God was not the surrender of a rich, meaningful life in order to grudgingly accept God's less-than-satisfying purpose. This was no capitulation to a second-best life for the sake of obedience. The life God has given me has been far more gratifying than what I'd envisioned for myself. While the creation of economic development through home construction is a good and worthy pursuit, God's call on my life transformed my ambition to a passion for creating a spiritual movement through the multiplication of disciples, something that is much more exciting and fulfilling to me personally. It was painful at the moment, but my surrender to God opened the door to a more fulfilling future than I had imagined for myself. I would not have experienced that had I not been willing to trust God at a deep level—not only with my career but also with my entire life.

Spiritual conflict occurs when our faith and feelings collide. Surrender is the act by which faith triumphs over feeling. The feelings preceding the moment of surrender are largely negative, so surrender often feels like losing. In fact it is quite the opposite. Surrender is a triumph of faith that ultimately produces gain. Jesus made that clear, saying, "Whoever wants to be my disciple must deny themselves and take up their cross daily and follow me" (Luke 9:23). That's the moment of surrender, which calls for faith to assert itself over feelings of anxiety, self-will, and the fear of loss. Yet, notice how Jesus immediately followed this call for surrender with the promise of a positive outcome. "For whoever wants to save their life will lose it, but whoever loses their life for me will save it" (v. 24). Clinging to our own ideas about life, cowering in fear of surrender, refusing to go with Jesus down a narrower path—all of this results in a greater loss: the loss of opportunity for growth and fruitfulness. In the moment, surrendering to Christ feels like a sacrifice, even a loss, but it opens the door to a far deeper experience of life.

To grow in spiritual maturity and ministry fruitfulness, you must redefine the term *surrender*. Scratch out the definition that reads "painful act of contrition that leads to a diminished sense of self and a limited future," and write in this correction:

"the resolution of a spiritual conflict by the joyful acceptance of God's perfect will, leading to a deeper level of maturity and greater kingdom effectiveness." When you learn to view surrender properly, the act may still arouse conflicting emotions, but you will be enabled to respond with faith.

Growth Comes through Listening and Reflecting

The interior conflict surrounding my call to ministry taught me another vital lesson about surrender: the critical importance of listening carefully to discern the voice of God amid many others. That discernment often comes through time spent reflecting prayerfully on the events of one's life. While I am grateful for my grandmother's prophetic confirmation of my call to ministry, I was right in thinking that her voice was not the one I should follow. Amid the cacophony of voices from family, friends, coworkers, church members, the broader culture, and even my own thoughts, I had to find a way to discern the voice of God. That has been an ongoing point of growth for me, but willingness to tone down other voices and tune in to the Spirit's leading is the critical starting point for that discernment. The practice of listening for God's voice has played a crucial role in each major moment of my life, and I'm grateful to have discovered that need early in life. To respond faithfully to the spiritual conflicts in your life, you must cultivate the practice of listening for God's voice through daily spiritual disciplines and theological reflection.

Over time I have seen the cycle of conflict, listening, surrender, and growth played out in my life. Because I grew up in a home with godly parents and was deeply rooted in the church, many of these moments came early. As a seven-year-old child, I asked Jesus into my heart. I remember kneeling at the altar in the Berkley Hills Pilgrim Holiness Church and feeling a bit embarrassed because the little girl kneeling nearby might notice me wiping away tears. However, faith (my trust in Christ) overcame feeling (my embarrassment). I was able to hear and respond to the voice of God. That childhood surrender altered my eternal destiny. Yet at the age of seven, I could not be fully aware of the implications of that decision or how it would later affect my life. It would take years of spiritual reflection to understand that moment in a deeper way.

Reflecting on later moments of conflict and surrender I've experienced, I plotted these instances on a timeline of my life. I can see that my initial surrender to Jesus at age seven, and even my deeper commitment to serving Christ vocationally at age eighteen were both complete and incomplete surrenders. While I had surrendered all that I understood God was asking of me at the time, I could not know what further spiritual challenges would come to me or the deeper ways in which God would call me to surrender my will, attitudes, and ingrained patterns of thought and behavior. As I reflected on these moments of significant spiritual conflict in my life and the deeper level of surrender that they produced, I began to think of them as *offering plate moments.* That term may call for a bit of explanation.

Jesus said, "For where your treasure is, there your heart will be also" (Matt. 6:21). That simple statement exposes a deep spiritual truth, one we intuitively affirm even

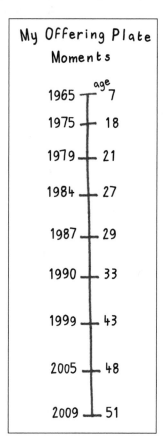

My Offering Plate Moments

year	age
1965	7
1975	18
1979	21
1984	27
1987	29
1990	33
1999	43
2005	48
2009	51

though we may wish to deny it: Our use of money reveals our deepest values. That's what makes the offering during a worship service either a moment of blessing or conflict for each worshiper. Those who have surrendered their finances to God most often find joy in the opportunity to give. Those for whom personal finances remain a point of struggle may find themselves feeling conflicted or anxious when the plates are passed. As I reflected on my experiences of spiritual conflict and surrender, the image of an offering plate came vividly to mind. I could almost envision myself feeling greater and greater resistance as the offering plate of God's call moved closer and closer to me. Finally, I could see myself putting not money but my whole self, once again, into the offering plate as an act of surrender to God. I surrendered my "treasure" (all that I was) to God's call. Just as the opportunity to give comes regularly during worship services, I've found that occasions that call for a deeper level of surrender come periodically throughout life.

Not all significant moments are surrender moments, however. Many significant events have been deeply moving for me and have altered the course of my life: moments like my marriage to Jan, the birth of our children and grandchildren, educational experiences, and the death of my father. I could name many more. Yet those were not moments of surrender for me. While they have been important and meaningful, I have grown the most spiritually by engaging in and reflecting back on the opportunities for surrender God has placed before me.

It's also true that defining moments occur in the context of daily moments. I begin nearly every day by reading God's Word, praying, and writing in my journal. Many of these daily moments seem very ordinary, but their cumulative effect is powerful. Some people live only for the dramatic, defining moments, but skip the daily disciplines. They become experience junkies, craving a spiritual high while ignoring the daily spiritual exercises that set the stage for victory. This can lead to a roller coaster of ups and downs, twists and turns. Jesus calls his disciples to "take up their cross *daily*" and follow him (Luke 9:23, emphasis added). By praying, imbibing Scripture, fasting, journaling, meditating, and engaging in other daily disciplines, we learn to make sense of the more dramatic moments when they come.

Surrender requires both listening for God's voice and reflecting on our spiritual experiences. Without a willingness to hear from God and the cultivation of that practice through daily spiritual disciplines, the offering plate will likely pass you by. You simply will not be aware of the challenge God has placed before you, or you may fail to appreciate its value even if you initially respond with faith. Listen for God's voice and reflect prayerfully on your life experiences, and you will be better able to accept moments of surrender when they come.

The Critical Question

The term *offering plate* may bring to mind a variety of images. You might think of a brass saucer with a red velvet lining. Perhaps you're used to seeing cloth bags with wooden handles, quart-sized pails, or even KFC buckets. Younger readers may wonder what an offering plate is because they have contributed to a church only through a website or smartphone app. The point is that not all offering plates look alike. In the same way, not all offering plate moments are identical. My timeline of surrender reveals God's unwillingness to be tamed or predictable, to be limited by what I expect. I have learned that I cannot stereotype what surrender looks like or what prompts it. I must simply be alert for the voice of God in my life.

The same is true for you. As you read a number of my offering plate moments throughout this book, one danger is that you will try to draw an exact parallel to your experience. It may not be there. God works individually in our circumstances but also universally through the call to deeper commitment, which produces emotional conflict that a new level of surrender resolves.

In Old Testament times, God ordained different types of sacrifices to be offered on different kinds of occasions. Some were to atone for guilt, others to display devotion or gratitude, or to acknowledge God's sovereignty. My offering plate moments have risen from a variety of life circumstances and have called for the surrender of different areas of my life. Your awareness of God's calls for surrender will rise from your increasing intimacy with God, not through a greater ability to predict the timing of his work. Walking closely and courageously with Christ, entering into deep relationships with others, and carrying out God's work in the world will put you in a better position to discern his voice and heed his call for surrender. My experiences may serve as an example of one who has done that, but the timing, circumstances, and specific calls to surrender will certainly be different in your life.

At age eighteen, I surrendered to Christ at a deeper level than I previously had done. My call to ministry resulted from and led to a deeper sanctifying work in my life. That work empowered me to love God with everything that I am and to love my neighbor as myself—a perfect love that fulfills what Jesus identified as the greatest commandment. That work also positioned me to serve his church and fulfill his mission from a heart purified by receiving his love and by channeling that love to others. It transformed my life.

All of that began when I found the faith to respond to the one question that Jesus asked then and has continued to ask at various points in my life: "Do you believe that surrendering to me is best for you?" Can you answer that yourself?

Position vs. Passion

IS YOUR PLACE OF
SERVICE DETERMINED
BY YOUR POSITION
OR YOUR PASSION?

April 1979

"So what advice would you give to a new pastor looking for a first ministry assignment?"

During my last year at Marion College (now Indiana Wesleyan University), I found myself in a one-on-one conversation with Laurel Buckingham, pastor of a fast-growing congregation in Moncton, New Brunswick. I wasn't about to pass up the opportunity for some free mentoring, so I cornered him for an impromptu conversation. In just ten years, Dr. Buckingham had led a church of one hundred people to reach out in innovative ways. The congregation, then numbered well over nine hundred, was on its way to a high mark of more than two thousand attendees.

Pastor Buckingham was dressed in a pinstriped double-breasted suit, his signature wardrobe. I was wearing bell-bottom jeans and a T-shirt, my standard campus attire, but Dr. Buckingham didn't care. I've always been grateful for the moments he spent with me on campus, and for this bit of advice, which deeply impacted my thinking about ministry: "Pray that God will call you to a community where you could spend a lifetime."

Those words helped me to imagine a new vision for my work, and the deep impact that I might make on a community over a lifetime of ministry. I'd like to think of it as great faith, perhaps it was youthful idealism, but I began to pray with all my heart: "Lord, call me to a *place* where I can invest my *life*." What I could not foresee, however, was that it would take another crisis of faith, another offering plate moment, every bit as agonizing as the previous one, for that prayer to be answered.

Life was busy in those days, and my final year of college moved along at lightning speed. In addition to my studies, I served as part-time youth pastor at Westview Wesleyan Church, a congregation of about two hundred and fifty that was in a building program, just a ten-minute drive from campus. Carles Fletcher was the senior pastor, and his energetic style reminded me a little of my friend, Dick Wynn. Both men were full of good ideas. I was learning a lot, both on campus and in the church. Jan and I had been married the previous August, and that first year of marriage was happy but a little chaotic. She relocated from her lifelong home in Grand Rapids and took a full-time position as administrative assistant at Westview. We were making new friends and forming deep relationships that have endured to this day.

Time was ticking away, however, and the question of what to do after graduation began to feel more urgent. I knew I wanted to continue my education by attending seminary at some point, but I sensed it would be best to spend some time in full-time ministry first. During those months, three strands were forming themselves into a cord in my thinking. One was my entrepreneurial spark, something that exposure to leaders like Dick Wynn and Carles Fletcher fanned in me. The second was Laurel Buckingham's challenge to seek a place where I could invest a lifetime. I had a growing curiosity about the prospect of long-term ministry in a single community. The third was my growing interest in church planting, or starting a brand-new congregation.

At the time, I was convinced that the idea of starting a new congregation rose purely from my strong desire to win people to Christ and from my innovative mind-set. I now suspect that my youthful ego had something to do with it as well. I loved the church I grew up in, and I enjoyed working at Westview, both established congregations with a long history. Yet, I hungered to break out of what I increasingly saw as the limiting factors of an established congregation, and church planting seemed like the best way to do that. I wanted to make my own mark on the kingdom. Was that God's call or my own ego talking? I would soon find out.

Around that time I began meeting for prayer with my good friend, Dennis Jackson. Dennis and I had met during our first year as ministerial students and occupants of Williams Hall, one of the men's dorms on campus. We shared a creative, innovative outlook on ministry, and we were both facing imminent decisions about our future. We agreed to meet in Dennis's office on Friday mornings for focused prayer about the next chapter in each of our lives. I use the word *office* generously. Dennis and Gwen had a tiny apartment on Harmon Street, in which he'd converted a broom closet to a small office. So when I say his home office became our prayer closet, it was literally true. We met in that closet at six o'clock each Friday morning to seek God's direction. The fact that two college kids were out of bed, let alone holding a prayer meeting at that hour, says something about our deep desire to discern the Spirit's leading.

As we prayed together over a number of weeks and as I reflected on the promptings of the Spirit, I gravitated even more toward the idea of being called to spend a lifetime in one community. I was used to the idea that pastors were called by churches, so the idea that a pastor could be called to a *community* intrigued and excited me. The thought of being called for a *lifetime* also resonated with me. At that time, the average tenure for a pastor in my denomination was barely three years. I began to wonder what greater impact a pastor might make if he or she were to invest an entire career in a single place. The more I thought about it, the more I wanted to find out.

The fruit of those prayer times was a definite sense that God was leading more toward the community of Kentwood, a southeastern suburb of Grand Rapids, Michigan. I had grown up in Rockford, a small community north of Grand Rapids, and Jan had grown up on the northeast side of the city. Jan and I knew little about Kentwood other than it was on the growth edge of Grand Rapids. Kentwood was then a city of about thirty thousand, having grown by 50 percent in the preceding decade.

I also knew that Dick Wynn and his family lived in Kentwood and drove across town every week to attend our church in Berkley Hills. That limited familiarity was enough to plant a seed in my mind, one that I watered with prayer. I felt drawn to a community, not to a particular congregation. Since there was no Wesleyan church in Kentwood at the time, I would have to plant one, a project that could take a lifetime. And that strongly appealed to my entrepreneurial mind-set. It seemed that the three strands of my ministry cord were now firmly woven together.

Solomon teaches us that a cord of three strands is not quickly broken (Eccl. 4:12). A strong cord can also very easily produce a rope burn, and I was about to find out how difficult it is to hold one's plans tightly when they are in God's hands.

"That's him," Dennis said, as a powder-blue Cadillac pulled up in front of Dennis and Gwen's apartment. Vaughn Drummonds, superintendent of the West Michigan District was on campus for a recruiting visit. Vaughn had been Dennis's pastor in Battle Creek, and Dennis had asked him to meet with us, given that we both would be graduating and seeking ministry opportunities.

I have to admit I was a bit intimidated. At only twenty-one and not yet out of college, I was about to tell this ministry veteran that God had called me, Wayne Schmidt from Rockford, to plant a church in the fastest growing suburb of Grand Rapids. I had no idea how he would respond; I only hoped I wouldn't be laughed out of the room. We sat on the second-hand couch in the living room, and I explained the vision I thought God had put on my heart. I described my conversation with Laurel Buckingham and the challenge to invest my life in one community. I talked about the many hours of focused prayer Dennis and I had shared. I even related my call to ministry and my belief that God had called me to do something creative and entrepreneurial. "I've prayed about this intently," I concluded, "and I believe I've sensed the Lord's will for my future. I'm going to plant a church in Kentwood."

Vaughn stared at me for a long minute, a quizzical smile on his face. Then he threw his head back and laughed out loud.

I was too shocked to speak, which turned out to be a good thing. When he finished cackling, Vaughn told me the reason for his laughter. Just the week before he had been in the Kentwood home of his good friend, none other than Dick Wynn. Vaughn said that he had asked Dick to consider planting a church in Kentwood, but Dick said no because that would mean leaving the staff of Youth for Christ.

"But here's what I will do," Dick had said. "If you find the right young person to work alongside me as a full-time assistant pastor, I'll be the part-time senior pastor to help get the church started."

I had no knowledge of that conversation before meeting with Vaughn. It was obvious to him and to me that God was supernaturally arranging for that "right young person" to be me. But here's the burn. To accept this assignment, which was obviously the exact opportunity I had prayed for, felt called to, and that God had now placed in my lap, I would have to serve as an assistant to someone else. I would not be the senior leader. I'd be the gofer.

I would like to tell you that my first reaction to Vaughn's news was elation. I would love to say that I grinned like a kid in a candy store, that I cried tears of joy and was too humbled to speak and finally managed to choke out the words, "Thank you, Rev. Drummonds. I'm so excited I can't stand it." But that didn't happen. My face maintained the mask of a polite smile, but on the inside I seethed with frustration and jealousy. I had no desire to be an assistant anything. I had spent months pondering this opportunity, daydreaming about possibilities, and even sketching ministry plans. I had already begun to try on titles like senior leader and founding pastor. This was my vision, my calling, my opportunity, and I wanted to be the leader. I left the meeting agreeing to meet with Dick, but feeling certain that this was the end of my dream. The three strands of my ministry cord were unraveling even before I switched my tassel from right to left.

Other people's problems often sound a bit petty, and I'm sure my dilemma concerning my place of service seems that way to some. Frankly, it seems foolish to me, in retrospect. But the conflict was real. I should have been elated by the opportunity to serve under an experienced, visionary man who had coached countless young leaders. It was an ideal arrangement. I would be able to take kingdom risks without bearing the full weight of responsibility. I would continue to be mentored by the very person who had helped me navigate my call to ministry. Not to mention the fact that Dick had valuable contacts in the community that could help us in the early days. But I wasn't elated, and I gave clues to that when I met with Dick a short time later.

Hearing that I might be interested in coming on board with the Kentwood church plant, Dick invited me to drive down from Marion and meet him at the Indianapolis airport. He was on a layover en route home to Grand Rapids. We met in a coffee shop in the terminal. As Dick described his vision for the church, I realized that it was tremendously exciting and even more energizing than my own plans. But the question of ownership still gnawed at me. I wondered how long he intended to stay on as senior pastor.

"So, where do you see yourself in the next five years?" I asked, trying to couch my real question in a standard job interview query.

Dick wasn't fooled. He was too discerning and he knew my impatient temperament too well. Years later he would tell me that he'd envisioned the arrangement lasting only a couple of years, anticipating he would be promoted in Youth for Christ and move to Chicago, which is exactly what happened. He and Vaughn had even talked about grooming me to take over leadership of the new church. But as we sat in that restaurant, Dick clearly saw the ego and arrogance behind my probing questions.

"I don't have a definite timeline," Dick said. "I'll be there as senior pastor as long as the Lord needs me."

So there it was, offering plate moment number three. God was jabbing a finger into my over-inflated self-importance, and the pressure was excruciating. "Is your place of service determined by your position or your passion?" God seemed to be asking. Would I be willing to play only the one role I coveted in fulfilling God's mission? Or would I play any role he needed me to play—even the seemingly lowly role of an assistant?

I gave Dick no clue about the turmoil within me, but I was wrecked. I drove away from the airport knowing that I faced another moment that called for surrender. I could see that much of my motivation for planting a church was driven by position rather than mission. To follow Jesus more fully, I would have to surrender my craving for recognition. I would have to repent of the arrogance that led me to believe I was able to stand alone when I clearly needed further maturity and training. It is possible to serve oneself under the guise of serving the church, and I was being convicted of that motivation very early. A few years earlier, God had asked me to surrender my own plans for life to accept his call for ministry, and I was able to meet that challenge with faith. Now, God was calling me to surrender my ego in order to do the very work he had called me to. I saw that as clearly as I see the words on this page. Yet, I still didn't know if I could do it.

During the several weeks before graduation, the spirit of God worked within me. Gradually, he removed sinful arrogance while preserving the passion to use my personality, strengths, and gifts to advance the kingdom. I agreed to serve along with Dick as his assistant pastor. For the next two years, I had an amazing mentor who stretched me in ways I could not have anticipated. Dick's responsibilities with Youth for Christ took him out of town nearly every week, including about one quarter of the weekends. We established a pattern of meeting each Monday to look at what lay ahead. He coached me on the appointments, meetings, and major tasks, and upon his return we debriefed in detail. I flourished because of his strategic presence and his strategic absence.

The church had a stronger start and greater vision than I could have provided as a solo leader. Dick's ministry had taken him around the world, and he had spearheaded events that involved thousands of young people. His great faith became embedded in the DNA of Kentwood Community Church. Also, Jan and I had a couple more years for our new marriage to gain strength and intimacy before I assumed the significantly greater burden that came with being the primary leader. Having secondary responsibility for a time was much healthier for me and for our marriage. At age twenty-four, when I became the senior pastor of a growing congregation, I was much better prepared spiritually and professionally than I'd been just two years prior. My willingness to surrender the honor of first position was a significant growth step, and it drove home a truth that I, like so many others, had resisted: Surrender is a source of strength.

When Surrender Happens

....

THEREFORE, I URGE
YOU, BROTHERS AND
SISTERS, IN VIEW OF
GOD'S MERCY . . .

ROMANS 12:1

Surrender is a source of strength.

That's counterintuitive. We're shaped by a culture that respects power, so we have come to believe that power is its own fuel and surrender is a sign of weakness. We conceive of strength as a quantity rather than a quality. It is something we have stored up in a tank. This strength is our fuel, and any weakness is like a leak in the fuel line. It drains our strength. Accordingly, we think of the act of surrender as pulling the plug on strength.

To surrender is to drain the tank, leaving us powerless. That is certainly what I was thinking when I faced my offering plate moment in 1979. I believed that if I were to surrender myself to the leadership of another, I would be disempowered and useless.

As the Spirit worked in my heart, I began to wonder whether the opposite might be true. What if surrender, in spiritual terms, is not the opposite of strength but is actually its source? What if strength is not a substance that fuels us, but a quality that defines our outlook, our spiritual health, our very lives? That actually is the case, though it requires some reorientation to see the truth that strength is found in weakness. We find strength in submission, not in domination. Humility, not hubris, is our gateway to strength. Surrender is not the drain in our tank. It is what opens us to God's sufficient grace. When we reach the point of surrender, we are where God can unleash his grace in our lives in ways we hadn't thought possible. But how does that moment come about? What brings us to an offering plate moment? When does surrender happen? Simply put, surrender occurs when our level of urgency ("I urge you, brothers and sisters") is combined with understanding ("in view of God's mercy") and results in sacrifice ("present your bodies"). Let's examine that dynamic, starting with a simple paradigm that I call the Grace Grid.

The Context for Grace

Early in my spiritual journey, I discovered that I understand spiritual truth best when I can relate it to some spatial or mechanical process. Perhaps that's the repressed construction engineer within me, or maybe I'm a visual learner. Either way, I like to sketch on paper the work I see God doing in my heart. My journals are filled with hand-drawn diagrams of spiritual discovery—and so is this book. I hope these sketches will help you understand God's spiritual work in concrete terms.

Our surrender to God combined with our expectation of his response opens the door to his grace. Consecration and expectation provide the context for receiving God's grace, which results in our strengthening for Christlike living and effective kingdom service. We can picture that dynamic like this.

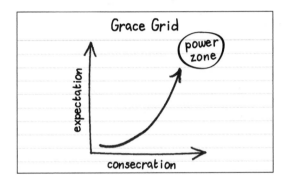

Expectation

Our expectation level is the first critical factor in this process. We have a tendency to live up or down to the level of our own expectations. Just as water seeks its own level, so we will experience the grace of God in our lives more or less according to the level of our expectations. If we don't expect God to do much in us or through us, he won't. When we do expect God to release his grace into our lives, he will. Setting expectations is critical for any human endeavor, and spirituality is no different. A coach knows athletes will not win a game they expect to lose, so the coach inspires her players to expect victory. Expecting more of ourselves, and even more important, expecting more from God, lifts the lid on our faith and positions us to go beyond what we might achieve on our own. When our sights are on the floor, we're unlikely to see the work God is doing, or wants to do, in the world and in our future.

For years I pastored in a community where a significant percentage of the population had grown up in a faith tradition that taught them this prayer: "Forgive me today for the sins I commit in word, thought, and deed." Initially I was struck by the humility of those who offered this prayer in a way that went beyond mere habit. It is admirable to recognize the need to repent of sin and receive forgiveness promptly, even daily. Yet, as time went on, I realized that this prayer shaped the expectations of many who prayed it. They came to believe that sin would be a routine aspect of every believer's daily life. There was no way to avoid sin. In fact, to receive anything good from God, you had to sin first. God's grace was available for forgiveness only, not for resisting temptation.

One of the perspectives I've most deeply appreciated in my Wesleyan tradition is its optimistic view of grace. Grace can strengthen us for victory over sin. This goes beyond mere behavior modification to true transformation. This powerful grace enables us not only to recover from defeat, but also to live in victory. It positions us to experience a greater fullness of God's Spirit, to be cleansed, empowered, and enabled to join him in transforming the world. One of my favorite prayers recorded in the Bible portrays that optimistic view of grace. It is the apostle Paul's "power prayer" recorded in Ephesians 3:16–21. Just reading these words raises our expectation of the power available to us through the Father, Son, and Holy Spirit.

> I pray that out of his glorious riches he may strengthen you with power through his Spirit in your inner being, so that Christ may dwell in your hearts through faith. And I pray that you, being rooted and established in love, may have power, together with all the Lord's holy people, to grasp how wide and long and high and deep is the love of Christ, and to know this love that surpasses

knowledge—that you may be filled to the measure of all the fullness of God.

Now to him who is able to do immeasurably more than all we ask or imagine, according to his power that is at work within us, to him be glory in the church and in Christ Jesus throughout all generations, for ever and ever! Amen.

Paul's prayer expands our expectation of the dimensions of God's love for us. It is wider, deeper, and more powerful than anything we can imagine. The apostle wanted us to be filled with this love "to the measure of all the fullness of God," a measure that is beyond our comprehension. Our expectations should be raised considerably by now, but there is more. Paul took it up another notch by pointing to the object of his prayer, the God who "is able to do immeasurably more than all we ask or imagine" by the power that is "at work within us." To this God be "glory in the church and in Christ Jesus throughout all generations, for ever and ever! Amen."

Wow!

God's power at work in you surpasses knowledge. Through it, God is able to do more than you could possibly ask for. This is a possibility greater than you know, greater than you can even imagine. If your expectations have not risen yet, go back and reread Paul's prayer. When you grasp this truth, it'll blow your mind.

Low expectations can be a lid on your faith. They limit the grace you receive, the power you experience, and the level of effectiveness of your spiritual life and ministry. However, expectation is only one part of the equation. The second critical aspect is the consecration of your life to God, your surrender.

Consecration

Judson W. Van Deventer's classic hymn, "All to Jesus I Surrender," was part of the soundtrack of my early church life.

Many of us sang these words countless times at the close of worship services, revival meetings, and youth camps. These lines capture the essence of the concept of consecration:

> All to Jesus I surrender, All to Him I freely give;
> I will ever love and trust Him, In His presence daily live.
> I surrender all, I surrender all;
> All to Thee, my blessed Savior, I surrender all.[1]

I surrender all. I suspect most of us would be more comfortable with an updated version of that hymn that adjusted the obsolete "all". We would probably be more inclined to sing, "I surrender most." Or perhaps "Some, to you, my equal partner; I surrender some." Rather than consecrating our lives, we usually compartmentalize them. We section off areas of life for God's control, usually the things we're least emotional about, and retain control of the things that matter most. We want much from God, but we seem unwilling to surrender much of ourselves in return.

That approach is just as limiting as having low expectations. Expecting little from God and surrendering little to God results in receiving little from God. To access God's grace and experience his empowerment, we must expect him to give that grace and consecrate ourselves in order to receive it. If I have high expectations and low consecration, I will receive only a fraction of God's available grace. When I am self-centered rather than Christ-centered, surrendering only the remnants of my life rather than every realm shows that my high expectations are all about me and what I want, not about God's purposes. In that case, God won't trust me with the grace and power he desires to give.

When we have great expectations of what God will do and fully surrender our lives, consecrating them fully to him, the conditions are right for God to act. We are positioned to receive his grace, and the result will be that we have the power to live and serve God in ways that will glorify him and impact the world for generations to come.

So if expectation and consecration provide the context for receiving grace, when do those grace points occur? Where are the specific points at which God works in our lives?

Grace Points

Grace is God's work, not ours. We surrender ourselves to God and expect great things from him, but those actions are really reactions to God's grace. He is the one who provides grace in the form of forgiveness, cleansing, empowerment, spiritual fruit, and the ability to serve in his kingdom. In nearly every case, that flow of grace into our lives coincides with a step of faith on our part. We can think of these steps as ascending stairs on a staircase.

Stepping Up

We think of surrender as a lowering of ourselves, and it is in some sense. Paul traced that downward movement in the life of Jesus, who, being God, humbled himself to take human form and even submitted to the indignity of death on our behalf. Yet by lowering himself in that way, Jesus achieved an even greater exaltation as "God exalted him to the highest place" (see Phil. 2:5–11). So the "step down" from heaven was really a step up into the fullness of the Father's plan and power.

The same can be true for us. When we surrender ourselves to God, it feels somehow like downward movement. We have less control of our lives. It seems limiting, like a demotion, a step down. In fact, stepping into God's grace is always a step up. Scripture identifies various ways that people respond to the grace of God and the result that response produces. Each successive response requires a greater degree of surrender. In that sense, it requires a step down. However, each step down results in receiving a greater measure of God's grace and power. In that sense, it is a huge step up. Picture it like a staircase.

The top step refers to Stephen, who was so full of grace and power that he did great wonders and signs among the people (see Acts 6:8). That text echoes John's description of Jesus himself, who came from the Father "full of grace and truth" (John 1:14). What if Stephen had been only half-filled with grace? What if he had been open to receiving only some of the grace God would have poured into his life? It's hard to imagine he would have been the effective leader in the early church we know him to have been, or that he would have submitted to martyrdom, the literal surrender of his life.

We know Jesus faced the temptation to hold back part of himself from the Father's will. That was the essence of his temptation in the wilderness and his choice at Gethsemane. Would he reserve control over his ambition, his ego, his physical appetites, or his instinct to survive? Or would he surrender himself fully to the Father's will and plan? As the writer of Hebrews reminded us, it was because of Jesus's "reverent submission" that he became the Savior of the world (Heb. 5:7-9). The step down in obedience is always a step up to grace and power.

Stepping Into

We can picture levels of grace as ascending steps, and I have described my most grace-filled experiences as offering plate moments. However, God is continually at work in our lives and our experience of grace is not always prompted by great crisis. We can picture grace in stages, which may last for some time. Our crises or moments of sacrifice may be dividing points between stages of grace or milestones within them, but growth in grace also has a progressive quality. We step into grace at various points in our faith journey. Without it, we could never come to know Christ, receive the gift of salvation, or grow to maturity.

**Being Filled
with Grace**

Results in
Power
(Acts 6:8)

Patient Suffering

Leads to
Abounding
in Grace
(1 Pet. 1:2)

Giving

Leads to Excelling
in Grace
(2 Cor. 8:7)

Obedience

Results in
Growing in Grace
(2 Pet. 3:18)

Humility

Leads to
Receiving More
Grace (James 4:6)

Stubbornness

Results in Missing
God's Grace
(Heb. 12:15)

**Using Grace for
Selfish Purposes**

Brings
Condemnation
(Jude 4)

Prevenient grace describes God's work in reaching out to us, even before we are aware of him. The apostle Paul put his finger on this when he wrote, "But God demonstrates his own love for us in this: While we were still sinners, Christ died for us" (Rom. 5:8). If God had not loved us and reached out to us with forgiveness, there could be no talk of either salvation or growing in grace. Through God's grace, we receive the ability to know God, to place our faith in him, and to respond to his love with the surrender of our lives. Many people make steps in grace even before they are aware of what is happening. God softens their hearts, melting away prideful self-sufficiency so they can turn to him for salvation.

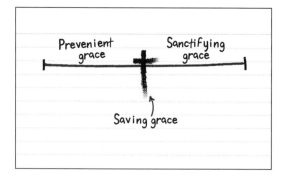

Saving grace is something more. Prevenient grace draws us to Christ, but saving grace is the regenerating work of the Spirit in our hearts. As John put it, "Yet to all who did receive him, to those who believed in his name, he gave the right to become children of God" (John 1:12). This is the point at which we consciously respond to God's grace with faith. When we place our trust in Christ, God's power is released into our lives and we are born again, as Jesus described it (3:3). This is the point at which many are tempted to stop the process. Having surrendered their past to Christ, confessing sin and asking for-giveness, they believe the grace journey is complete. Others, sensing that even greater levels of surrender will be required in the future, are tempted to halt in their tracks. This was my temptation upon receiving my call to ministry. I knew that an additional level of surrender was required, and I rightly perceived that there was much more on the line than my choice of career. The dynamic of grace and surrender must be ongoing in a believer's life. And that brings us to the next stage of grace.

Sanctifying grace describes the work of the Holy Spirit in bringing believers to maturity. Here is where the grace moments become most intense. As we are prompted by the Spirit to greater levels of surrender (the horizontal axis on the Grace Grid) and expectation (the vertical axis), God's grace can operate in our lives in an exponential fashion. You may notice I have not placed a moment of entire sanctification on the timeline above, and the Grace Grid pictured earlier is open ended. That's because there is no end to our need for ongoing surrender or for greater levels of expectation. No matter how we would describe our level of maturity in Christ, there is always room for growth in sanctification. What we may have believed was "complete" consecration at one moment in our lives may, in retrospect, appear to have been incomplete. We surrendered all that we knew at the time. But as we receive more grace, we see new areas that must be surrendered to God.

If we were to plot these moments or steps on the Grace Grid, it might look something like this.

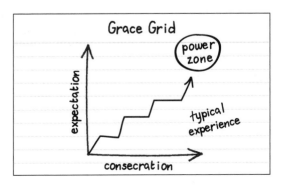

Each of the turning points or steps on our Grace Grid would represent moments, large and small, when God prompted us to surrender more, expect more, and receive more from him. Some would be critical junctures, offering plate moments that called for a major, purposeful reconsecration of our lives. Others might be smaller points at which we choose faith over fear, obedience over obstinacy, or humility over pride. In each case, a point of surrender paired with a new expectation of what God will do results in a higher level of power in our lives. We take a step forward in faith, and God lifts us higher in grace and power.

Knowing this pattern, why don't we take grace steps more often? What accounts for the lengthy gaps between our moments of greater surrender? To answer that question, we must understand the cycle that characterizes nearly every type of change, especially spiritual growth.

The Cycle of Discontent

Change rarely happens without a sense of urgency. That may be why Paul wrote with such earnestness about the issue of consecration in Romans 12:1, "Therefore, I urge you." A holy discontent precedes every grace step, leading us to adopt a new perspective (greater expectation) and take a new step of faith (greater consecration). Without that sense of discontent, of urgency, we would likely delay our spiritual growth until "someday." Discontent prompts change today. And when that sense of discontent collides with a fresh understanding of truth ("in view of God's mercy"), we become even more responsive to God's leading. We recognize that his (prevenient) grace is leading us to an opportunity for greater devotion. So spiritual change follows a pathway that looks something like this.

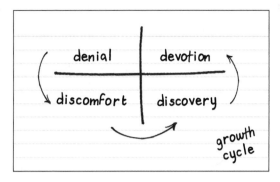

This growth cycle begins with denial. When the Spirit prompts us to see new truth and surrender at a deeper level, our first response is usually, "Problem? What problem?" That was my first response to my call to ministry in 1975. "That's just Grandma Cole talking," I assured myself. I was in denial that God was even speaking to me, let alone that I needed to take some action. It requires some level of surrender even to admit there is a problem.

Discomfort is the second stage of the process. This is the holy discontent that will not allow our spirit to rest until there is resolution. Without question, this is the most painful aspect of the cycle of grace. Though our inner feelings are screaming for change, we have no clear direction in which to act. The pain is even more acute when there is both internal and external resistance. That is, when we have personal feelings of discomfort and uncertainty combined with pressure from others and our need to please them. In these moments, it's tempting to retreat back to the relative comfort of denial. The willingness to remain in this discomfort is by itself a form of surrender. When we are willing to allow ourselves to feel that holy discontent, to feel the fear, uncertainty, and anticipation of loss, we are cooperating with the Holy Spirit at some level as he draws us forward.

Discovery is the third stage of the cycle. It occurs when we accept the fact that some change must take place and we therefore surrender ourselves to God's time frame of bringing clarity. We engage in learning about ourselves, about the future, about the consequences and rewards of possible actions. Engaging this process is something like sending the twelve spies into Canaan. It is a time of patiently exploring and evaluating to determine God's will. During this time our expectations are raised. We come to see that new, better things are possible through God's grace.

The cycle ends with devotion, or a new level of surrender and a new outpouring of God's grace. We surrender ourselves first to God (consecration) and then to his specific will (obedience). This takes us to a new level of power for personally living the life of Christ and for serving effectively in his kingdom.

To the question of why we don't take more grace steps or take them sooner, the answer is we are not ready. We have not developed the holy discontent that will break us free from denial, enable us to endure the discomfort of anticipating change, explore the will of God, and, finally, surrender ourselves to him in obedience. Offering plate moments are moments of significant spiritual change that require a deep work of the Spirit. We place ourselves in a position to experience them by saying yes to God in smaller ways that move us through the cycle of denial, discontent, and discovery toward a new moment of devotion. When we embrace them, these moments of deep surrender lead us to a previously unimagined experience of God's grace and power in our lives.

God's Work

One danger in mapping the movement of grace in our lives is we come to think of it as a mechanical rather than an organic process. If we can see it on paper, we may believe we can control it somehow. We might think of the Grace Grid as a kind of vending machine for God's power. It is not. Remember God is the actor in this process, and we are reactors. No moment of surrender comes without him first leading us to it by his prevenient grace, or drawing us deeper and deeper by his sanctifying grace. Sanctification is not something you can do on your own, and it certainly isn't something you can control. This is God's work.

After my offering plate moments in 1975 and 1979, I was beginning to get a handle on the Grace Grid. I could see the relationship between my willingness to surrender to God's will and the release of his grace in my life and ministry. I had embraced the idea that surrender leads to power. However, I had yet to learn that human strength was totally inadequate for effective ministry. I would learn that lesson through a fourth, and even more painful, offering plate moment that came just five years into my ministry at Kentwood. This moment would test me at an even deeper level, the level of my true motivation for serving God.

Driven vs. Called

CALLED PEOPLE
POSSESS STRENGTH
FROM WITHIN,
A QUALITY OF
PERSEVERANCE
AND POWER THAT
ARE IMPERVIOUS
TO THE BLOWS
FROM WITHOUT.

December 1984

Planting a church is like push-starting a car that has a dead battery. First, put the car in neutral and push to get it rolling. If there's a slope handy or if you have a few friends nearby, that helps. Otherwise, just get behind it and heave with all your might. Once you gain a little momentum, run alongside and hop into the driver's seat. Hopefully, it's not moving so fast that you can't get in or too slow that it won't start.

As quickly as you can, depress the clutch, put the car in gear, then pop the clutch so the engine is forced to cycle. Don't forget to turn the key. With any luck, the engine will fire, and off you go. Otherwise, get out and try again. When you get home, look for a gentle slope to park on. Tomorrow you'll do this all over again.

By 1984, I had repeated that process, figuratively speaking, every day for five years. Starting Kentwood Community Church (KCC) took a tremendous amount of time and energy, and I gave it every bit I had. Sometimes our little church rolled along pretty well, and sometimes it seemed to stall. In either case, I simply worked harder. I was determined to see this church succeed. Why? Because God needed a church in Kentwood, and I needed to plant one there.

In the early days, we met in a school. That's commonplace for new churches now, but in those days it was unheard of. In the conservative culture of Grand Rapids, having a facility meant credibility, and we had neither. Though we made some gains each year, those gains were small and hard-won. After four years, we had pushed our way to an average attendance of about one hundred sixty.

On the positive side, every person who came was highly committed. Everyone pitched in one way or another. Some set up chairs, others played in the worship band, others led a small group. We had lots of help pushing the car. What we didn't have was control over the school thermostat. Wherever the custodian set it on Friday afternoon was where it remained on Sunday morning. We froze all winter and baked all summer. Other than the auditorium, the only room available to us was the teachers' lounge, and in those days teachers were allowed to smoke on school grounds. That room became our nursery! To this day, when I smell the pungent odor of stale cigarette smoke, I think back to my arriving at Valleywood Middle School on Sunday morning to set up for church.

In 1981, Dick Wynn was promoted to national leadership with Youth for Christ and moved to Chicago, leaving me as the senior pastor. Though Dick was a hands-off leader, he was a valued mentor, and I felt the loss keenly. We had lots of volunteers, and by the middle of 1982, we even had an energetic young assistant pastor named Kevin Myers. Yet, I began to feel increasingly alone. The burden of leadership weighed heavily on my shoulders. I was the senior pastor after all, and I had so much to prove. I needed to prove that I, at just twenty-four years of age, was capable of leading a church. I had to prove I could preach sermons that would be meaningful to the young professionals who lived in our community. I needed to prove we were the right church for young families who showed up, looking for the best place to introduce their children to the faith. So I wrote sermons and planned worship services, followed up on newcomers, coached volunteers, and networked in the community. If KCC were to fail, it wasn't going to be my fault. I would plant this church or die trying.

During much of 1983, I even served as a construction worker. We had been able to purchase a 6.4-acre plot of land on Eastern Avenue and begin to build a permanent church home. The finances were extremely tight, which added another layer of stress. My dad served as the general contractor, and we volunteers did nearly all of the labor. On Sundays, I would set up, preach, and then tear down at the elementary school. On Mondays, I would swing a hammer or unload supplies on the construction site. It felt as if I were doing it all, pushing and pushing and pushing to get KCC moving all by myself.

And then it happened.

On a Sunday in August 1983, we held the first worship service in our new facility. Attendance doubled on that very day. The old car had finally bumped to a start, and it took off at full throttle. New people started coming every Sunday, many of them suffering through difficult life circumstances such as divorce or addiction. People experiencing hard times found themselves unwelcome in many of the area traditional churches. Word had begun to get out about this upstart congregation on the south side of Grand Rapids. "Go to Kentwood Community," people said. "They'll take anybody." And we did. We adopted the motto, "Growing by Loving," and that's exactly what was happening. For four years, I'd been pushing with all my might to gain a little momentum. In year five, we popped the clutch and took off like a shot.

Yet, there was a downside. Just a few weeks earlier, we had been an all-volunteer church. Now we were a church of mostly spectators. There had been no creature comforts at the school, so the consumers stayed away. But as I looked out over the congregation in our new facility, I realized there were many there who had come to enjoy the sacrifice of others. A lot of them eventually bought into the Kentwood vision and made their own sacrifices to continue the mission, but they arrived as shoppers. These new folks came from a variety of religious backgrounds, or none at all, and they brought with them differing notions of what a church should or shouldn't be. For the first time, we had critics rather than cheerleaders.

Our worship leader, Marv Hollenbeck, was a talented, engaging musician who introduced contemporary music into our services. He led worship from the piano rather than the pulpit. In fact, we had no pulpit. I preached without notes and moved comfortably around the open platform. Our Sunday evening divorce ministry grew to over one hundred fifty people, and we reached out to the community in other imaginative ways also. We hosted our own version of *Saturday Night Live*, which we called *Forever Family*. It was a quirky, fun variety program of skits and music that became extremely popular in the community and solidified our reputation as an innovative congregation. Some people wouldn't miss it; others thought it was too irreverent to be held at a church and vowed not to return. While those activities may seem ordinary today, in the mid-1980s, they put us on the cutting edge—or out in left field, depending on whom you talked to. Newcomers sometimes criticized our music on their very first Sunday. Outsiders routinely mistrusted our methods. Even some members of my own denomination questioned whether KCC was a "real church."

Yet we kept growing, and within a year after relocating, we had outgrown our 7,800-square-foot facility and took out another construction loan, at a double-digit interest rate, to add space. That meant more meetings, more decisions, and more financial pressure. And the newcomers kept coming. Every week, there were more people I had to win or woo or witness to, recruit or retain, or fire up or calm down, or otherwise convince that KCC was the place for them. Around that time, I led our volunteers in a spiritual gifts discovery course, but I was pastoring as if I held all the gifts and others had none. It was exhausting.

By the summer, I was nearing the end of my rope. Jan and I took our two preschool boys on a getaway to Lake Geneva, Wisconsin. Lake Geneva is a lovely resort town just northwest of Chicago, lined with beautiful lake homes and lovely village shops, but I saw few of the sights and spent very little time on the water. I slept much of every day and had little energy for what remained. "Something has to change," Jan said, as we loaded up the car to head home. "We can't keep living like this."

I knew she was right, but had no idea how to make it happen. The church needed me. The kingdom needed me. And I, it seemed, needed to be needed. I was living on a hamster wheel, running, running, running every day yet always feeling farther behind. As we loaded the kids into the car, I handed her the keys. "Will you drive?" I said. "I'm just too tired."

As if I didn't have enough to do during those early years of ministry, I had enrolled in a master of arts program at Calvin Theological Seminary in Grand Rapids. Along with attending classes there, I often used the library for sermon preparation. It seemed the one place of calm in my increasingly turbulent life. Toward the end of the fall semester in 1984, I noticed the book *Ordering Your Private World* by Gordon MacDonald, which was new at the time

I'd been running on fumes for well over a year, and as I began to read, I easily recognized myself in MacDonald's description of a disordered life, especially in the distinction between being driven and being called.

> "How can you spot a driven person?" MacDonald asked.
>
> "Today it is relatively easy. Start with the signs of stress, and you have probably found some driven men and women. . . . Many in our society are under constant and destructive stress as life for them operates at a pace that offers little time for any restorative rest and retreat. . . . People worked hard in the days of my child-hood, very hard. But they generally knew when to stop working. . . . Sure, people got tired. But they didn't constantly complain of the exhaustion we hear about today. Has it occurred to you how often we talk about our fatigue?"[1]

"Ouch," I thought. "Nailed me on the first try." I kept reading.

"Driven people often project a bravado of confidence as they forge ahead with their achievement-oriented life plan. But often, at the moment when it is least expected, adversities and obstructions conspire, and there can be a personal collapse. Called people, on the other hand, possess strength from within, a quality of perseverance and power that are impervious to the blows from without."[2]

I put the book down, close to tears. "That's it," I said to myself. "That's the life I want."

MacDonald's words had broken through my denial about the life I'd been living and the cost to myself and my family. My hard work—all the late nights and early mornings, the relentless drive to do more, achieve more, be more—was driven not by my love for the Lord nor even a sense of calling. All of it stemmed from a sense of insecurity. I was trying to prove my worth to everyone from first-time visitors shopping for church to my pastoral colleagues who were skeptical of my work. I was running from meeting to meeting, church event to church event, Sunday to Sunday, in a vain attempt to prove that I, Wayne Schmidt from Rockford, was capable of doing something meaningful in the world.

Not surprisingly, the growth of KCC did nothing to satisfy this hunger for significance. The church's growth only heightened my sense of insecurity because each person who came was one more person I had to impress in order to feel worthy. It left me physically exhausted, spiritually drained, and relationally bankrupt. I knew I was genuinely called to ministry, but this drivenness was not a sign of strength. It was a spiritual disease that threatened to end my ministry.

Sitting there in the reading room of Heckman Library, I realized another offering plate moment was upon me. I was overwhelmed by the need to surrender my mixed motivations to the Lord. Tears of relief began to flow as I realized freedom from this infinite loop of seeking and not finding was just around the corner. I felt relief also that this drivenness had not cost me my marriage, as it had so many others. Yet I felt fear as well, fear about my need to find forgiveness from my wife for my selfish inattention and fear about how to move into a new future.

For years I'd been giving Jan my emotional leftovers, scraps at best. She had been patient, but that patience was wearing thin. Over the past couple of years, she had occasionally tried to raise the subject of my workaholism, but I was too adept at rhetoric. I could outtalk her every time, often spiritualizing my overwork as a sacrificial gift to the Lord. Realizing conversation on this matter was pointless, she had left me several handwritten notes over the previous year, painfully confronting my neglect of our marriage and family. As I reflected on those messages, my defensiveness now gone, I clearly saw the pain I had caused her and the dangerous trajectory of our marriage. I was resolved to change, but I wasn't sure how.

My health was deteriorating also. The exhausting burden of trying to prove my worth by pleasing others had ruined my physical disciplines. I was twenty-five pounds overweight and had allowed no room in my schedule for basic self-care—rest, exercise, and other restorative activities. After years of addiction to adrenaline, I would need to learn to live, love, and lead in a whole new way, but I had no idea how to do it.

For years, it had seemed counterintuitive to me that truly loving people might mean not pleasing them, but I saw that truth clearly that day in the library. Pleasing people had interfered with my pleasing God. Genuinely loving God would result in a love for people that would put their interests first, regardless of whether they affirmed me for it. I had read the apostle Paul's declaration in Galatians 1:10 many times, and now I finally saw its power: "Am I now trying to win the approval of human beings, or of God? Or am I trying to please people? If

I were still trying to please people, I would not be a servant of Christ." I resolved that day to learn this lesson, one I have had to reaffirm a number of times since.

My five-year milestone ministry anniversary was not a time of celebration. It was a crisis that had been several years in the making. I'd hit the wall, coming perilously close to burnout in both ministry and marriage. I sought God's forgiveness. I knew I needed a fresh infusion of his unconditional love to break this bondage to pleasing others as a way of proving my worth. He went deeper still, exposing the root of my insecurity and my failure to find my security in him. "Lord," I prayed, "I'm giving it all to you. My ministry. The church. My marriage. All the people, all the expectations, all the need—I give up."

"I see this in myself now," I said to Jan, "and I'm going to change. No more putting others first. No more working crazy hours. No more neglecting you and the boys. I'm sorry for the way I've treated you. Things will be different from now on." She offered her forgiveness, and I rested in her embrace. I was grateful for her prayers and love as I was attempting to break this destructive cycle and find my adequacy in Christ.

After a moment, Jan looked up at me and said, "So how is this going to happen? What's going to be different, starting tomorrow?" It was a good question; one I had already been grappling with. I soon realized that consistent victory over the impulses of insecurity would come only with help from others.

I began 1985 with the resolve to start an accountability partnership. I approached Paul Anthes, a layperson in our church whom I respected highly, with an invitation to form such a partnership. Though different in many ways, we had a common intensity and intentionality about being fully devoted followers of Jesus Christ. We agreed that meeting every other week for prayer and accountability would raise our batting average in seeking first God's kingdom and righteousness. We each developed a top-ten list of goals to ask each other about. We could answer each question yes or no, indicating that we'd fulfilled the goal in the previous two weeks or not. After reviewing our goals, we asked each other this question based on Gordon MacDonald's book: "How is it with your private world?" Our initial meeting that January marked the beginning of an accountability partnership that has lasted more than thirty years and has helped me live in victory over the temptations that rise from insecurity.

In 1984, I had wanted to believe my call to ministry and the fullness of the Spirit I had experienced in earlier moments of surrender had eliminated my vulnerability to insecurity. That presumption led to denial about the mixed motivations that fueled my service to God. I did have a genuine call to ministry, but I had blended it with my need to prove my self-worth by gaining the approval of others. When I finally recognized that tendency and surrendered it to God, the Achilles' heel of insecurity was still there, but I was now aware of it and able to keep it surrendered. Nothing in the external environment had changed, but my inner spirit was different. I was finally able to believe I had nothing to prove, that God is sufficient for my ministry, for my marriage, for all of me. I am grateful for the freedom I have experienced, and I treasure the intimacy with Jan that was rescued from ruin through my willingness to surrender.

I still do not profess that my motivations are entirely pure. The human heart is a complex instrument, and it seems each of us has a personal drive that tries to alloy itself with God's purpose for our lives. Rather than declaring absolute victory over mixed motivations, we do best to keep vigilant in our area of weakness. When we see the temptation of people pleasing or longing for power or seeking wealth or whatever may be our particular struggle rearing its head, we must avoid denial, make confession, and seek accountability. That is what keeps us walking in victory.

The Pathway of Surrender

OFFER YOUR BODIES
AS A LIVING SACRIFICE,
HOLY AND PLEASING
TO GOD—THIS IS
YOUR TRUE AND
PROPER WORSHIP.

ROMANS 12:1

Reflecting on my brush with burnout in 1984, I was at first puzzled about why it had occurred. I had surrendered my life to Christ at a young age. As a teen, I had given my ambition to the Lord, gladly accepting his call to ministry. As a fledgling pastor, I had even surrendered my ego to Christ, accepting a subordinate role in my first assignment. Why then did I find myself struggling with insecurity? Why was I prone to workaholism? I had given that area of my life—career—without reservation. What had gone wrong?

It took quite some time, years actually, to realize, while I had surrendered that *area* of my life to Christ, I had not surrendered all *levels* of my life to him. My surrender was in the right context, ministry, but it had not worked its way through my entire being. Though I had given my heart to God, I was still operating by my own impulses at the level of my emotions and especially in my actions and reactions. In short, I was sacrificed on the inside but not on the outside. My surrender had not reached the level of my emotions, which were driving my actions.

This brings us to the question of the sequence of surrender, or how it makes its way through the various levels of our being. Surrender begins with the spirit, but it does not end there. Surrender must progress outward to encompass the mind and body. Entire sanctification is holiness in spirit, soul, and body.

Holistic Surrender

The apostle Paul gave us a clue to the holistic nature of surrender in Romans 12:1, where he urged, "Offer your bodies as a living sacrifice." We are more used to hearing the idea of surrender cast in spiritual terms. We give our heart to Jesus. We love God wholeheartedly. Yet Paul's described surrender in unmistakably sensual language. We give our *bodies* to the Lord. We surrender our sight, taste, smell, hearing, and touch. This holistic surrender is the appropriate response to God's mercy. We give him everything, and he fills us in body, mind, and spirit.

Paul presented this concept again in 1 Thessalonians 5:23–24, where he wrote, "May God himself, the God of peace, sanctify you through and through. May your whole spirit, soul and body be kept blameless at the coming of our Lord Jesus Christ. The one who calls you is faithful, and he will do it." Here we see the holistic nature of surrender stated even more clearly. Whatever aspects there are to your life—tastes, desires, affections, actions, reasoning, will, experiences—God wants to sanctify them all. And notice Paul's optimism about the outcome: God *will* make it happen.

Jesus's own words point us in the direction of holistic surrender. When asked about the greatest commandment in the law, he replied, "'Love the Lord your God with all your heart and with all your soul and with all your mind and with all your strength.' The second is this: 'Love your neighbor as yourself'" (Mark 12:30–31). Love for God must radiate through the entire person—heart, soul, mind, and strength. And it must extend beyond even that to the point of loving action toward others, something that must involve us physically in the realm of action.

God wants us to be devoted to him from the inside out. He wants our heart, yes. And from that transformed core, he wants surrender to radiate outward through every level of our lives. This is the pathway of surrender: spirit to soul, soul to body.

Let's define those terms a bit further. By *spirit*, I mean the inmost being, the seat of our affections. The word *heart* is a good synonym for this. The *soul* refers to our inner life, our self-concept, will, thoughts, intellect, and emotions. The term *mind* is a good synonym for this because so much of this soul activity has to do with our thoughts. The *body* is our physical self, our senses, experiences, and actions. Surrender moves in one direction only, from spirit to soul to body. A change of heart produces a change of mind. A change of mind produces a change in behavior.

The culture approaches life transformation from the opposite direction, working from the outside in. The culture generally begins with behavior modification techniques that attempt to change the way a person acts regardless of what he or she feels or believes. The hope is that emotions and beliefs will come along later. This is the "fake it till you make it" approach. Though behavior modification can be successful in the short term, it ultimately falls short. Adopting new habits and even repressing old thoughts may be effective for a while, but these outward acts can never penetrate the heart. And it is from the heart that good or evil works its way into our lives (see Luke 6:45).

In my younger days, teaching about surrender, holiness, or entire sanctification nearly always majored on behavior. We Christians were known for our moral conduct, not necessarily for our loving hearts. As a result, many of us younger folk could name a handful of adults who professed to be entirely sanctified based on their avoidance of certain behaviors, but whose emotions and ambitions were decidedly unaltered. They didn't smoke or drink or chew or go with girls who do, but they were mean-spirited and entirely unloving. Surrender doesn't travel from the outside in. They didn't understand that it moves from the inside out.

Paradigms of Surrender

We can picture this pathway in a couple of ways. One of the most helpful is the Worship Well. This diagram illustrates the levels of our being and the pathway surrender travels, welling up from the depths of our spirit to encompass the soul and senses. I first saw this diagram when Pastor Kevin Myers sketched it on a napkin years ago. He and worship leader Chris Morgan have used it as a teaching tool at 12Stone Church. I've also heard Chris talk about how this applies to corporate worship. We often think a sensory expression of praise is equivalent to authentic worship. Therefore, if we can engage people in standing, clapping, singing, moving, talking, or engaging in some other bodily activity, we will have succeeded in prompting true worship. As Chris points out, sensory expression is just the beginning. Worship must engage the soul with new thoughts, emotions, and choices, finally reaching the deepest level of the spirit. Then our love for God will well back up into voluntary expressions such as singing. Though worship may be prompted by a sensory experience, it must travel all the way to the heart or it will be meaningless. As Paul wrote, "If I speak in the tongues of men or of angels, but do not have love, I am only a resounding gong or a clanging cymbal" (1 Cor. 13:1).

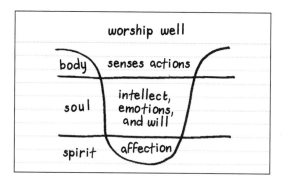

Another way to picture the relationship between these levels of our being is as a target. The spirit, not the senses or even emotions, is the bull's eye. That's what we're aiming for in surrender. The outer rings are easier to hit, but they don't win the prize. Likewise, changing one or two behaviors is far more easily done than surrendering one's whole heart to Christ. God wants the very core of our being. Only when we surrender will our love for him radiate outward to encompass intellect, emotions, senses, and actions.

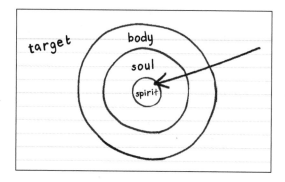

The Urgency of Surrender

As I discovered in 1984, surrender that doesn't flow outward to encompass the total person is not complete. We may believe we've surrendered ourselves fully to God because we've surrendered every area of life, as far as we know. However, if that surrender doesn't encompass spirit, mind, and body, it leaves us vulnerable to sin. We live in the realm of the senses and emotions. We feel angry or anxious, and that affects our behavior. We do things every day that can lead us closer to God's will for our lives or farther away. We'd like to think that a moment of surrendering the heart to Christ produces a surrendered life. It doesn't, unless accompanied by the daily acts of surrender that include the countless choices we make each day. Surrender must travel from the heart to the head and finally the hands.

Jesus made that clear in his strong statement about practical holiness in Matthew 5:29–30. "If your right eye causes you to stumble, gouge it out and throw it away. It is better for you to lose one part of your body than for your whole body to be thrown into hell. And if your right hand causes you to stumble, cut it off and throw it away. It is better for you to lose one part of your body than for your whole body to go into hell." We don't interpret those words literally. If we were to do so, I suspect many people would be missing an eye or a hand. Yet Jesus's command does communicate great urgency. Surrender is a matter of life and death. Our devotion to God must incorporate our total being—eyes, hands, and all.

A Matter of Life and Death

Paul unpacked this truth in Romans 6. First, note the contrast between what we might call half-surrender or incomplete surrender and total consecration. Paul set up this contrast with two rhetorical questions: "Shall we go on sinning so that grace may increase?" (Rom. 6:1) and "Shall we sin because we are not under the law but under grace?" (Rom. 6:15). This permission mentality is a clear indication of partial surrender. Apparently, Paul encountered that kind of thinking in Christians of his day. Today, this thinking shows itself in statements like "Christians aren't perfect, just forgiven" and others implying that surrender of the heart is all God desires. Our emotions, senses, and actions are not important. We're abounding in grace and free from the rigid constraints of the law, so what we actually do is of little consequence, right? "By no means!" is Paul's emphatic response (Rom. 6:2–15). Throughout Romans 6, Paul explained why that permissive, half-surrendered life is so dangerous.

First, Paul urged us not to offer ourselves as instruments of wickedness (v. 13), and then he wrote that we must offer "every part" of ourselves as an instrument of righteousness. Consider that word *offer*. What image comes to mind, especially paired with the word *instrument*? You might think of a soldier handing over a bayonet. Or you might envision a surgeon, reaching out to grasp a scalpel offered by an assistant. It makes a world of difference into whose hands the instrument is placed. In one set of hands, the blade is an instrument of death. In another's, it is an instrument of life. In spiritual terms, we either offer ourselves— every part of ourselves—to Satan or to God. Neutrality on this subject is a myth. The idea that we can be masters of our own fate is an illusion. We will be "used" by something or some- one, either for good or for evil. So, Paul asked whether we will continue to believe our behavior is of little consequence, essentially offering "our bodies" as instruments of death? "By no means!" Surrender must encompass the total person or it is not surrender at all. Anything less leads to death.

Positive and Negative Surrender

I am of the generation that rebelled strongly against the many behavioral constraints some Christians had attached to the idea of surrender. Making lists of behaviors Christians must always do or never do invariably degenerates into legalism, and we were right to throw that off. However, Paul was willing to state a couple of firm dos and don'ts that accompany surrender. While he wisely stopped short of naming specific behaviors, his statements show the surrendered heart must work its way out into surrendered behavior.

The "don't" statements came first. "Do not let sin reign in your mortal body so that you obey its evil desires. Do not offer any part of yourself to sin as an instrument of wickedness" (Rom. 6:12–13). Both imperatives are based on a previous decision to "count yourselves dead to sin" (v. 11). Both verbs used, *reign* and *obey,* speak to the issue of control. We have surrendered ourselves either to sin or to righteousness, Satan or Christ. One or the other will wholly own us.

Also, note the phrases "in your mortal body" and "any part of yourself." They remind us we're talking about the whole person. Paul's concrete language did away with the idea that a spiritualized surrender was good enough. We are talking about the whole person—spirit, mind, and body. The micro term, "any part," seems to indicate that certain body parts (perhaps eyes and hands, as identified by Jesus) are especially prone to trouble.

Let's apply Paul's thinking to the common situations you or I might face on any given day. Though your specific list might vary, we could discover that offering ourselves to righteousness looks something like this.

- Don't place yourself near a person of the opposite sex in ways that may lead you away from your spouse emotionally.
- Don't look at websites that tempt you with pornography.
- Don't walk into the mall if you have trouble with over-spending and debt.

- Don't hang out with friends who pull you into ungodly behaviors.

There is great power in proximity. When you place yourself near something or someone, you are more likely to come under its influence. In some cases, the sin seems to come near to us. Years ago, pornography was available only in certain stores. A person had to go there, ask the person behind the counter for it, and show proof of age. That process made it much easier to avoid. Now pornography is available to anyone with an Internet connection and can be viewed anonymously. We can more easily express anger or unkind thoughts through social media. We can more easily overconsume junk food because it is more and more available, and in larger portions. Each of these cases calls for a greater surrender of the mind and body. We may not wish to offer our bodies as instruments to sin, but sin continually offers itself to us. To live out the surrender we've made in the heart, we must exercise our will and emotions, sometimes removing ourselves from the proximity to temptation. Full surrender means avoiding sin.

Paul also gave the positive command, "[Do] offer every part of yourself to him as an instrument of righteousness" (v. 13). It helps to think of this offering of the whole self in specific terms. Paul said to offer *every single part* of yourself to God for his use. How might that play out in your life? What would it mean to offer your eyes to God? How might he use your sense of sight for your good and his glory? What would it mean to offer your ambition to God? Your art? Your speech? Your sexuality? Your labor? Paul's micro language forces us to think about specific actions. We must consider how the surrender of our heart to Christ will play itself out in the countless things we do in the course of a day. Surrender of the body must be done daily.

Surrender and Ownership

Moving further into Romans 6, we see that surrender produces a result in our lives. When we are fully surrendered, we enter a new state in that we are "slaves" to righteousness. Remember that the image of a slave in Paul's day was a bit different from ours. We think of slavery in terms of human trafficking, in which people are cruelly abused and exploited, often for sexual purposes, or we think of the slavery practiced in America in the nineteenth century, in which African American people were treated unconscionably. Without justifying the practice of slavery then or now, we can acknowledge that slaves in Paul's day were more likely to receive better treatment but lacked the ultimate freedom to choose their own destiny. This is the key point in Paul's mind. A slave was bound to carry out the will of his or her master. Slaves were not in control of where they lived or what they did each day. Someone else made those choices. When we sin, we come under the control of sin, just as a master controlled a slave. However, when we surrender to Christ, we become "slaves" to righteousness. As we'll see, that holds very good news for those who struggle to be free from sin.

Obedience Indicates Ownership

Paul pointed out that we become "slaves" to whomever we obey (vv. 16–17). We may be slaves to sin or slaves to righteousness, but it will be one or the other. How do you know which? Simple. Look at your behavior. What we say or even what we think is not proof of ownership. When it comes to surrender, it isn't the thought that counts. Who (or what) controls your actions? Greed? Insecurity? Lust? Anger? That is an indication of your ownership, just as are peace, forgiveness, tolerance, and love. Don't offer yourselves as slaves to sin any longer, Paul urged us. You've been liberated from that. Let your behavior reflect your obedience to your new master, Christ.

Here's an example of how obedience is a primary indicator of ownership. Jan and I enjoy taking our dog, Fletcher, for walks in the park. Though I say he is "our" dog, Jan is his primary caretaker. She feeds and grooms him; all I do is let him out occasionally and pet him once in a while. When we take Fletcher away from home, I can control him only by using a leash. When he spies a squirrel, or gets the scent of a rabbit, it sometimes takes a hefty jerk on the collar to bring him back to attention. Jan, on the other hand, can control the pup with a single word. He knows her voice, and he obeys it. That is the clearest test of ownership.

Obedience Becomes Normal

Thinking of obedience as slavery may make the act of surrender seem forced. It is as if we're grudgingly made to do something we really don't want to do. While that might be true in the beginning—we usually resist surrender at first—it isn't the case in the end. As Paul wrote, "You have come to obey from your heart the pattern of teaching that has now claimed your allegiance" (v. 17). Outward conformity is mere legalism. That's what happens when we try to work surrender from the outside in. You can force yourself to obey, at least for a while, but that will never change your heart. Your religion will be nothing but rules, and obedience will always be a duty. True surrender is wholehearted. Chris Bounds has said that Christians can be liberated from willful sin and empowered to live lives of obedience to Christ, but they can be set free from the inner propensity to rebellion, selfishness, and pride through the work of the Holy Spirit orienting their hearts to God. This is truly good news to those who have grown exhausted from an ongoing internal war, who have felt they did not have the inner resources to be fully devoted followers of Christ but have longed for the fruit of the Spirit. Victory is possible. Full surrender of the heart, though daunting at first, soon becomes wholehearted devotion. When that deep love for God radiates outward into the mind and body, obedience becomes normal.

Obedience Brings Freedom

Have you wondered why so many people continue in behaviors that are obviously harmful to their well-being and make them miserable? Perhaps you've wondered this about yourself. Why are bad habits so hard to break? Why do we repeat the same mistakes over and over again? Why do we do harmful things even while acknowledging they are foolish? One reason is that sin has a powerful hold on the life of an unsurrendered person. Remember we are slaves to sin. Breaking free from that slavery requires something more than a rational decision. It requires surrender to a new master. Paul exposed this dynamic with the rhetorical question, "When you were slaves to sin, you were free from the control of righteousness. What benefit did you reap at that time from the things you are now ashamed of? Those things result in death!" (Rom. 6:20–21). As slaves to sin, we're stuck in pointless, even harmful, behaviors.

Yet, when we choose a master, we gain the consequences that come with that choice. This is the meaning behind Paul's often-quoted statement, "For the wages of sin is death, but the gift of God is eternal life in Christ Jesus our Lord" (v. 23). Read in context, we see the full meaning of this powerful verse. The death resulting from sin is not simply a punishment imposed by God for violating a law. It is the natural result of being enslaved to a lousy master. It is the "reward" you get for choosing sin.

Fortunately, this work-and-wages analogy has a positive side as well. When we surrender ourselves fully to God, that surrender works its way out into our mind and body. We begin to think and act differently. That's because we are bound to a new master, and doing that master's will becomes more and more natural to us. And "the benefit you reap leads to holiness, and the result is eternal life" (v. 22). The law of cause and effect now works in our favor. Slavery to sin produces suffering, but slavery to God results in life.

The idea of proximity comes into play here also. When we are bound to sin, we are far from God. That distance prevents his Spirit from working within us. We are slaves to sin, so it is inevitable that we do sin. Obedience to God is not possible. Yet, as we allow ourselves to be "enticed" by righteousness and practice the spiritual disciplines, we come into proximity with the Spirit. As he works within us to complete our surrender through the pathway of heart, mind, and body, obedience becomes possible. We are now free *not* to sin. While there is never a state in this present life where Christians are immune from temptation, the ongoing bondage to sin can be broken. We no longer have to obey it. Though we sometimes struggle and will always be subject to weakness and infirmity, we are set free from the power of sin by God's grace. With sin, there is danger in proximity. With God, there is danger in distance. We gain power through our proximity to him through the Spirit. Through the Spirit, we gain freedom.

No Partial Surrender

There is no power in partial surrender. Surrender must apply not only to all areas of life, but also to all levels of the person: spirit, soul, and senses. According to legend, when the Russian ruler Ivan the Great converted to Christianity, his soldiers converted with him. However, the church at that time did not allow professional soldiers to be baptized. As a compromise, the soldiers were baptized by immersion, but each held his right arm out of the water. So each was fully consecrated to Christ—except for his sword arm.

Many Christians today attempt this kind of partial surrender, devoting nearly everything to God, but reserving one part of themselves for their own control. That kind of surrender is never effective. Either Christ will have all of you, or you will continue in slavery to sin. There is no middle way. When you surrender your whole heart to Jesus, that surrender will work its way into your inner life of thoughts, will, and emotions, and finally into your public life of actions, experience, and behavior. So the question is never "Have I surrendered this area of my life to Christ?" but rather "Does Christ have all of me?"

Scarcity vs. Generosity

**THE ONE WHO
GIVES IS THE
ONE WHO GAINS.**

March 1987

"You want to do what?"

I knew perfectly well what he'd said, but I needed time to think before responding. I was sitting in a corner booth at Mr. Burger with Kevin Myers, my assistant pastor of some five year's duration. We'd just come from an early morning workout at the YMCA and were having breakfast at one of Kentwood's more value-priced eateries.

"I want to plant a church in Atlanta," Kevin said again.

"This year." He paused, maybe for effect. "And I'd like to recruit some people from Kentwood Community Church (KCC) to go with me."

I took a long slurp of coffee, but realized I was running out of delaying tactics. I had to say something.

"Well, let's pray about it," I offered.

"I have prayed about it," Kevin said. "I'm ready to go. And I'm asking for your blessing. And financial support. I'd like to raise pledges from the congregation."

Maybe Kevin thought my nodding head was a gesture of affirmation. It wasn't. My mind was spinning and I had to do something to slow it down.

"I can't lose Kevin," I thought to myself. "Not with the new building—and the mortgage. We need every able body we've got, and *every dollar*."

"Well," I said again, "let me pray about it."

Some readers will recognize Kevin Myers as the founding pastor of 12Stone Church in Lawrenceville, Georgia, one of the largest and fastest growing congregations in the country.[1] In the spring of 1987, Kevin was just twenty-six years old and discipleship pastor at KCC. That 12Stone flowered under his leadership came as no surprise to me. I'd known Kevin since we were kids together at Berkley Hills Wesleyan Church. Our parents were good friends, and though Kevin was a few years younger than I, we got along well. When he graduated from

Marion College in 1982, I hired him immediately. KCC averaged only about one hundred fifty at the time, but I believed it would soon grow, and I could easily see Kevin's passion for disciple making and his leadership qualities.

From the start, Kevin had talked about his desire to plant a church in the Atlanta area, where he had some family connections. "I'll give you two years," he'd told me in 1982. When two years stretched into three, then five, I kept my mouth shut. This young leader had seemingly boundless energy, and though he was, well, unvarnished, I knew that his hard work and passion were fueling much of our growth. People were responding to his strong relational skills and unwavering call to discipleship, which included no-nonsense teaching on stewardship. Kevin strongly believed in tithing, and he taught that value to our congregation.

That teaching coincided with our desperate need to increase our financial base. Our congregation was growing by leaps and bounds, and our facilities just couldn't keep pace. We had outgrown our original building on Eastern Avenue in one year. We added space there, but had to add yet again the following year. Each project included more debt, which pushed us financially. By 1986, we had acquired a fifty-acre property on 60th Street Southeast and begun to build what is the church's current home. We moved into that new space in January 1987, just weeks before my conversation with Kevin. Though by then we were drawing more than a thousand worshipers each week, it didn't feel like we had an abundance of anything. Staff, time, finances, volunteers—everything was stretched tight like a rubber band. I felt sure that pushing even one resource a tiny bit further would cause us to snap.

Kevin's presence was a value to me personally as well. In our early days, still meeting in the rented school, we were both kids, laboring side by side and learning as we went. Strategy sessions were often held at Mr. Burger after our morning workouts. Kevin would pepper me with questions about our vision and next steps. I would often respond, "Good question, let's talk about that some more," then scramble to come up with answers before our next meeting. As a leader, I was learning every step of the way, and Kevin's inquisitive nature and constant drive pushed me to think and grow. It was good for me.

So there we were, both under thirty years of age, leading a church that had grown to more than a thousand people and we had just undertaken a major relocation project and the debt that came with it. As I reflected on the situation, a fresh wave of insecurity came over me. This was not the people-pleasing urge I'd dealt with a couple of years before. This feeling was rooted in the fear of failure. Will we have enough money? Can we survive the loss of a key leader? What if the whole thing falls apart? That fear drove me to one of the most crippling thought patterns for any leader: a scarcity mind-set. "Not now," I thought. "We can't let Kevin go just yet."

The decision wasn't up to me, of course, or even to the church board. But I did raise the matter with the board, and it came as no surprise to them. Kevin had frequently shared his vision with board members, most of whom were also friends.

"This is the beginning of our multiplying vision," one member said. "We've always wanted to be a church that plants churches."

He was right, of course, but my fear about losing a valued team member was clouding my memory.

"I'm just not sure we're in a position to let go of a key leader," I offered. "There's so much at stake right now." No one took that bait. The board seemed to have more confidence in my leadership ability than I did at that point. They didn't see that losing Kevin would slow us down.

After the board meeting, I thought about Kevin's plan. How many people would really be willing to relocate to Georgia to help start a church? Not many, I concluded. That conclusion was another sign of my scarcity thinking. As for the fundraising, I knew that would be a different story. Kevin was passionate and persuasive and deeply connected to people in the congregation. When he left, money would go with him. "Does he realize how tight things are around here?" I wondered. Our relocation had left us so strapped for cash we were considering not offering coffee before and after worship services. The ultimate sacrifice!

The longer I pondered the situation, the more this scarcity thinking took hold. "I just don't see how we'll make it." Sad to say, that was my internal response to Kevin's vision.

Within a few days, however, I began to feel troubled about the growing gap between my public and private rhetoric on the subject of generosity and multiplication. Years earlier, I had embraced the idea of KCC becoming a tithing church. I had cast this vision to our board and congregation. We would send out 10 percent of our congregation to begin a new church, then replace those members by making new converts. I had read somewhere that a healthy congregation should be able to produce converts each year at a rate equal to 10 percent of its worship attendance. So a healthy church of one thousand should make one hundred new converts annually. I reasoned that we should be able to plant a new church every other year and still be a growing congregation.

It all looked good on paper, and it had sounded good as I'd talked it up with our leaders. Somehow I never thought about the practical side of the equation—the impact on our leadership cadre, volunteer base, and cash flow. Perhaps I thought there would come a time when we weren't struggling to add space, when we were flush with money, overstaffed, and had more volunteers than we knew what to do with. As every pastor knows, that day never arrives. Now the test of my vision was upon us. Why did this tremendous opportunity suddenly seem like a burden? Why did investing in the kingdom feel like losing something? How had my vision for generosity, for planting, for investing in others so quickly degenerated into a spirit of scarcity?

I was facing yet another offering plate moment, and I knew it. "We'll never be a multiplying church unless I can cross this bridge," I concluded. The conflict went much deeper than the immediate issue of making a mortgage payment. God was calling me to trust him, in a new way, to provide. Did I truly believe that he is Jehovah Jireh, our Provider? Would I place my treasure—which I then measured in terms of staff members, attendees, and financial resources—in God's hands? Or would I keep them tightly under my control? Would my ministry, and my personal life, be characterized by generosity thinking or by a scarcity mind-set? Responding to Kevin's plan would be no one-time decision. This choice would shape the tone of my ministry from that day forward.

God's story, from Genesis to Revelation, is one of extravagant generosity. He expressed his love to us by freely giving his only Son. The great movements of redemptive history, each new chapter in his story, were brought about by actions that showed both courage and generosity. As I realized this, I began to see the smallness and ugliness of my thinking. The negative self-talk, the fear of losing momentum, anxiety about money—it appalled me. I laid all of it before my heavenly Father in prayer.

"Lord, you are the giver of good gifts. You are the Provider. You are the one who holds all things in the palm of your hand. And I trust you. I surrender my need for control. What few resources I have, I give them back to you. Multiply them, Father. Use them in any way you see fit."

By God's grace, I was able to realize that it truly is more blessed to give than to receive. In kingdom math, the one who holds on to his or her life, resources, treasure, is the one who loses. The one who gives is the one who gains. God's resources are beyond imagining. I was able to bless Kevin's plans to raise funds and volunteers within KCC. Publicly, I tried to be even more energetic about the venture than I felt. My heart surrender was still working its way into my emotions. I truly desired to trust God and bless the start of a new church. Intellectually, I had long ago made the decision to be a multiplying congregation, and I had reaffirmed that decision with an act of surrender. Yet I sometimes still felt a knot in my stomach when thinking about the future. No matter. I affirmed with my voice what my heart had chosen, even if my emotions were sometimes unstable.

"We believe in multiplying churches, and we want to bless Kevin," I told the congregation. "If you feel called to offer financial support, please be as generous as you can." Not surprisingly, one couple from Kentwood did accompany the Myers family to Georgia, and many others generously gave financial support. Each pledge both tested and reinforced my dependence upon a Father who knows how to give good gifts to his children.

Launching 12Stone was a test for me personally, and a test for KCC. Other tests would follow. Over the next two decades, KCC invested itself in a total of ten new congregations. In most cases, we contributed both people and money to launch each new church. When our members committed to being part of a launch team, we encouraged them to begin tithing to their new church home immediately because "where your treasure is there will your heart be also." We wanted their hearts to be fully invested in their commitment to form a new congregation.

As I look back over the thirty years God gave me to serve KCC, one of my greatest joys is the realization that KCC did become a multiplying church. God proved himself faithful every time the congregation gave of itself for kingdom purposes. In fact, when reviewing the attendance records from 1987 to the present, it is impossible to identify the years when people and money were sent out because God so quickly and generously replaced those resources. What would have been the cost had I been unwilling to sacrifice my desire for control in order to invest in the start of that first church plant in 1987? I'm grateful that God brought me to a new place of surrender and enabled me to move from a scarcity mind-set to an abundance mind-set. My own life, and I believe the lives of many others, have been greatly impacted as a result.

Where Surrender Stalls

DO NOT CONFORM
TO THE PATTERN OF
THIS WORLD, BUT
BE TRANSFORMED
BY THE RENEWING
OF YOUR MIND.

ROMANS 12:2

We've seen that surrender begins with the heart, the seat of our affections, and must travel to the soul and senses, mind, and body. Unsurrendered levels of our being, that is, parts of ourselves that we withhold from God, will eventually become gateways to sin, just as my desire to please others resulted in workaholism, which I confronted in 1984. As Paul put it, we must "offer every part" of ourselves to God (Rom. 6:13). That sounds easier than it is. Nearly everyone who has attempted this act of complete surrender has found that one level of our being nearly always becomes a roadblock. Though we have surrendered our heart to God and we desire to bring our behavior into obedience, something stands in the way. That something is what we have labeled the *soul*, our will, thoughts, and emotions. Paul refers to this as "your mind" in Romans 12:2. Between your heart (your capacity to love) and your senses (your capacity to act) stands your soul (the capacity to think, feel, and choose). That's where surrender often gets stuck.

This was my tipping point with the 12Stone Church launch. I had made the decision to lead a church multiplication effort through Kentwood Community Church (KCC). That was my heart. But my mind-set was rooted in frugality. I'm a fiscal conservative by nature, and I grew up in a culture that emphasized disciplined spending. When faced with the challenge of giving resources to a new congregation, my conservative thinking easily recruited the emotion of fear to create a scarcity mind-set. I had the right heart, but my mind was pulling in a different direction. Before long, I had rationalized a million reasons why I couldn't follow my surrendered heart into generous actions. I needed a change of mind.

This is exactly where Paul led in his description of surrender. It isn't enough to "offer your bodies" as a living sacrifice, because you won't be able to follow through on that sacrifice if you continue with old patterns of thought and feeling. In order to live this transformed life, you must break with the old patterns by renewing your mind.

Again, this is the reason behavior modification techniques are seldom effective in transforming a person. You can keep your behavior in check only as long as there are external constraints in place. When your mind and emotions are free to set their own course, they will trump your self-discipline every time. This is not to say that there is no interplay between senses and soul. What happens in life ripples into the soul. Your experiences do affect your mind (thinking), will (choosing), and emotions (feeling). The point is that these inner aspects of your being ultimately drive behavior. You will not live out your surrender so long as improper patterns exist in your soul.

So how do we break with the world's patterns so we can be renewed? Let's begin by identifying the three key aspects of soul: mind, will, and emotions. Note that in this chapter we'll avoid using the term *mind* as a synonym for soul because the mind, as the capacity to think, is a key component of this larger aspect of our being.

Being Renewed

Earlier in Romans, Paul indicated that overcoming sin involves an act of the mind and an act of the will. To "count yourselves dead to sin" is a thought (Rom. 6:11). And to "not offer any part of yourself to sin" but "offer every part of yourself to him" are choices you make (v. 13). In Romans 12, Paul made these same distinctions. We are to "not conform to the pattern of this world," which indicates choice. Instead, we are to be transformed by "renewing of your mind," which points to our thought patterns (12:2). When we're able to submit thought and volition to God, we will be in a position to know and do his will.

This is the same pathway we've seen before: thoughts drive choices and choices determine behavior. From our own experience, we can add a category along with mind and will, or maybe as a subset of mind, which is emotion. So we might alter our pathway slightly to say that thoughts drive feelings, feelings drive choices, and choices determine behavior. When surrender stalls in our lives, it's usually at the intersection of these three elements: mind, emotions, and will. Let's explore the dynamics of renewal in each of these elements of the soul.

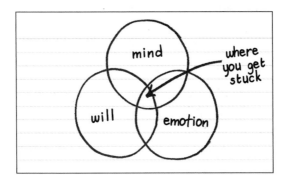

Renewing the Mind

The *mind* is your capacity to think. This is one of the most basic elements of our personhood. It is what makes us independent creatures. We can think before we can express those thoughts, as you may have observed in very young children. Infants and toddlers are capable of forming thoughts they can communicate only as facial expressions, physical reactions, or nonsense syllables. As we grow, we learn to think in certain ways. We develop thought patterns. I grew up in a community that emphasized thrift, and I learned to think conservatively about spending. That became a pattern of thought for me, which has generally been healthy. We appropriate or learn other patterns of thought regarding everything from sexuality to race to politics. Often, these thought patterns exist at a subconscious level. We're not aware we even have them. These are the thoughts our minds default to when it comes to any given subject. They may be right or wrong, harmful or helpful.

- Spending is bad; saving is good.
- A woman's place is in the home.

- It's good to experience new things.
- An eye for an eye, and a tooth for a tooth.

These patterns are the thoughts we hold without examining them. They're like the operating system on your computer. You never see it, but it determines how every program on your device will operate. These patterns drive our feelings and choices in ways we're not aware of. And that would be fine except for one thing: they're often wrong.

Our thought patterns too often conform to the pattern of the world, which is based on self. We all seem to be born thinking more is better, revenge is sweet, and other people exist to make us more comfortable. To renew the mind, you must identify and break the patterns that conform to the world's thinking.

A second aspect of our thought life is *reason.* Reason is our capacity to make sense of things. We do that by applying logic and analyzing information. Generally, reason is a good thing. However, we all know that our reason can be co-opted by our thought patterns and emotions. When that happens, we engage in rationalization. That's what I did when presented with Kevin's request to recruit people and funding from KCC for the launch of 12Stone. Although others could easily see this lined up perfectly with our vision and was an opportunity rather than a problem, my thought pattern drove me to fear, which produced a myriad of rationalizations like these: We can't afford it. It'll kill our momentum. We're already understaffed. At that point, my intellect had become a roadblock to surrender. Poor thought patterns combined with rationalization produced resistance to surrender.

Renewal of the mind comes through recognizing and rejecting false thought patterns and rationalization, and by growing the capacity to think in godly ways. There are many tools for doing this, though they likely fit into these three broad categories.

Learning. Renewing the mind depends on knowing the truth, and that involves learning. When we learn, we grow. Reading, new experiences, training, and other learning activities produce the aha moments that enable us to recognize old patterns and accept new information. When you learn, you further your ability to surrender.

Spiritual Disciplines. To renew the mind, it is not enough to explore the world or even your own thoughts. You need God's voice to speak into your thought processes. Prayer, Bible reading and study, silence, meditation, spiritual reflection, fasting, and other disciplines provide occasions for God to reveal truth to your mind. This squelches rationalization and helps you form new thought patterns.

Community. Other people can be a mirror for the soul. They often see us more clearly than we see ourselves. An accountability partner, small group, family members, or church family can help you identify negative thought patterns and call you on rationalization.

Renewing Emotions

Your *emotions* are your capacity to feel. Most of us are all too well acquainted with our emotions. They have the ability to drive us in negative ways even when we're aware of what's happening. You may know you are reacting from irrational fear, giving in to a jealous urge, or going too far in your anger, but that knowledge may leave you powerless. Our feelings seem to take control whether we want them to or not.

Often, we have default ways of responding emotionally that are very much like thought patterns. These emotional patterns, which we are often unaware of, can catapult us to certain actions without thought or even a conscious act of the will. When A happens, we respond with B based on emotion. Renewing the soul means identifying and changing our negative emotional responses and replacing them with good patterns. The good news hidden in this is that, once disciplined, our emotions can serve us very well. They can propel us toward obedience every bit as well as they drive us toward sin.

What are the tools for renewing this area of the soul? How do we identify and break conformity with the world at the level of our emotions? First, renew your mind. Our thought patterns often drive our emotions, so breaking bad patterns in the mind is a starting point for bringing emotions under control. Beyond that, here are two ways to renew your emotional life.

Love the Right Things. Many of our negative emotions are rooted in an unbridled love of self. We care most about ourselves, and when we feel threatened or insecure, our emotions go haywire. Think of the most powerful negative emotions you feel or the situations in which you get most emotional. Generally, they arise from occasions when you feel threatened. We feel abandoned and that results in jealousy. We feel insecure and that produces fear. We feel left out and that produces loneliness. We feel wronged and that produces anger or thoughts of revenge.

What would happen if our highest love were for God and others, not for ourselves? Our emotions would then come into the service of Christ and his kingdom. We would feel anger about injustice toward others. We would feel hatred of sin. We would feel jealous for the reputation of Christ. When we love God first, our emotions drive us toward obedience.

Practice Self-Awareness. When you feel an emotion, question it. Ask: What am I feeling? Why am I feeling this way? Often, that simple act of examining yourself will lead you to identify misplaced emotional reactions. If you are honest with yourself, you can often diagnose your own misaligned emotional patterns and move beyond them—or seek the help of others in doing so. Self-examination played a big part in the renewing of my mind from fear-based scarcity thinking to mind-set of abundance and generosity. I first had to identify the insecure feelings that drove my negative thought pattern.

Renewing the Will

The *will* is your capacity to choose. For many people, this is the primary point of attack in renewing the soul. We jump straight to our capacity to choose and attempt to strengthen our willpower. That often fails because the renewal is not holistic. We may make right choices, but without the right thoughts and emotions to back them up, that willpower quickly dissipates. It's a short-term fix at best.

Our will, too, is often driven by patterns, which we call habits. When a certain behavior aligns with our mind-set and emotional structure, we often continue it with no further act of the will on our part. Habits are behavior patterns that, once established, bypass the will altogether. Once established, they are incredibly difficult to change. Renewing the will is possible, however. Even long-entrenched patterns or habits can be changed. For most of us, the best way to renew our will is to work primarily on renewing our thoughts and emotions. In general, our thinking drives our emotions, and our emotions heavily color our choices. However, there are important things you can do to affect your will directly.

Subordinate Your Ambition. By ambition, I mean our ultimate aim in life or our highest goals. The default setting for ambition is to advance self, and that's where it remains for many people. While we may love God and desire to serve him, that love smacks up against our ambition to advance our own goals and reputation. Selfish ambition nearly always wins that battle. As with righting your emotions, the way to right your will is to redefine your highest goal. When your love for God is primary, your desire to advance his kingdom will be primary as well. This doesn't mean that you never feel a sense of achievement or do anything that benefits you. Rather, you subordinate your ambition to God's will, and you find that the desires of your own heart are satisfied in the process. As Jesus said, "Seek first his kingdom and his righteousness, and all these things will be given to you as well" (Matt. 6:33). Surrendering my ambition to God by accepting his call to ministry has not led me to frustration over my "lost" career as a real estate developer. Instead, I have found even greater satisfaction by serving in the way God directed.

Challenge Yourself. Willpower alone will not renew your soul. However, it can be a strength-building exercise, like lifting weights. When you feel the Spirit prompting you to take action, do it. Paul did this, as seen in his statement in Romans 15:20: "It has always been my ambition to preach the gospel where Christ was not known, so that I would not be building on someone else's foundation." Having surrendered his ambition to Christ, he was able to act on that ambition in bold ways. He set audacious goals, and he achieved them. Make a resolve and follow through on it. Set goals for yourself spiritually and personally. As you achieve them, your ability to make choices and act on them will be strengthened.

Seek Accountability. I've already mentioned my long-term accountability partnership and the positive effect it had on breaking poor behavior patterns in my life and replacing them with good ones. Having even one person hold you accountable for the choices you have made will increase your ability to enact them. Accountability is like a brace. It can't replace your will, but it can certainly reinforce your willpower when it weakens.

Identifying Your Soul Strength

When it comes to renewing the soul (*mind*, in Paul's terminology), there seem to be three types of people: thinking people, feeling people, and action people. Obviously, we all possess the capacity for each of the three aspects of the soul: mind, emotions, and will. However, it appears that one element is dominant over the others in a great many people. That explains why there is no easy formula for surrender, especially in this area of breaking conformity with worldly patterns.

Also, all of these aspects of the soul are interrelated. While it is generally true that thinking shapes emotion, which then drives choices, there is so much interplay between the three elements that this formula cannot be considered a hard-and-fast rule. Doubt (a thought) can be rooted in stubbornness (the will). That was my experience in questioning my call to ministry back in 1975. Reading the book that questioned the historicity of Christ's resurrection was not the cause of my doubt. The book was merely the fuel my mind used to stoke the conflict that had already arisen in my will.

Are you a mind, emotion, or will person? Some people are driven by intellect and seem to struggle less with emotion or will. Once they have new information, process it, and form a way of thinking, their emotions and will seem to follow along. Others are driven by emotion. Facts matter less to them than how they feel about a situation. This is not to say they are anti-intellectual or ignorant. Rather, emotion is their driving force. When they feel right about something, they make the choice to move forward. Such folk are often willing to take bold action or assume great risk for the kingdom. Still others are people of resolve. While not ignorant of facts, they seldom get bogged down by overthinking. Once they have made a choice, they are able to ignore or deal with emotions and follow through. Your complete surrender may be aided by knowing which aspect of your soul is most prominent. That's where your primary battle will be fought.

In addition to identifying your most active dimension, pay attention to the least-used aspect of your soul. Beware of leaving that undeveloped. Like many of my generation, I rebelled strongly against what I perceived to be the emotionalism of my revivalist heritage. I determined that I would not be manipulated at the level of my emotions and shut down that aspect of my being as it related to God. As a result, I failed to surrender my emotions to the Lord. I simply didn't consider that part of my spiritual life. That led to the struggle with insecurity that threatened my ministry and marriage.

With a bit of thought, you can probably identify the dominant feature of your inner life. What about the soul characteristics of your corporate life? Do marriages have a dominant soul trait? Do organizations? I'm convinced the same patterns that can develop in an individual can be present in relational groups. To be fully renewed, you may need to pay attention to the soul patterns in the social context of your life. There may be patterns there that either help or hinder your surrender.

In marriage, it is often said that opposites attract. If so, does that hold true in the context of soul strengths? What is the dominant soul characteristic of your spouse or family members with whom you closely interact? That strength may help you identify and move beyond unhealthy patterns in your own life. For example, if you are driven by emotion, but your spouse is shaped largely by intellect, you may balance one another. You can help your spouse identify overthinking or rationalization that prevents moving to choice. He or she may be able to spot the emotional defaults you cannot see in yourself. If you share the same weak areas, you will at least understand one another's struggle and can provide objectivity.

Denominations, and even local churches, often develop around a single aspect of the inner life, which can prove to be a weakness. Intellectually-driven people have a way of flocking together, as do those oriented toward decisive action and those who use emotion as a primary test of decision making. What is true for an individual is true for an organization: overdependence on any one of these aspects of the spiritual life can lead to error. Church leaders should engage people through each of the three dimensions of the inner life. At KCC, I made it a point to ask these questions at every worship planning session:

- What new insight are we communicating?
- At what point in the service will people feel moved by their participation?
- What challenge or call to action are we presenting?

Worship should involve the total person, and that includes all aspects of soul life—mind, emotions, and will. By leading people to engage all dimensions of their being, we aid them in making a complete surrender to Christ.

The Double-Souled Person

The apostle James added to our understanding of soul surrender when he wrote about the double-minded person (see James 1:8; 4:8). The word translated "double-minded," more literally, double-souled. The term describes a person whose loyalties are divided, one who has not fully decided to trust God, surrender completely, and live God's way. In his description of the double-souled person, James perfectly described the tension of living the half-surrendered life.

First, this person lives in a state of indecision. Though God promises wisdom to all who seek it, the double-souled person can expect no such gift nor the certainty that comes with it. This person is filled with doubt, tossed this way and that, unstable in every way (1:5–8). You may be able to relate to this description. In your heart, you want to surrender fully to God, but your emotions pull you in different directions. Or you rationalize one behavior, then another, unable to make a decision. The problem is a divided soul—mind, emotions, or will. The solution is complete surrender, bringing all aspects of life into harmony with God.

That internal chaos can overflow into relational chaos, which James later described. Since double-souled people are not completely honest with themselves, they are not open with one another. They harbor secret desires that lead to jealousy, insecurity, envy, bickering, and even violence (4:1–2). Though they do pray, these folk receive nothing from God because they harbor a selfish motive. They purport to be seeking God's will, and perhaps even believe they are, yet their true aim is self-interest (v. 3). Echoing Paul's thought that a person must be wholly owned either by sin or by God, James pointed out that double-souled people seem ignorant of the fact that they must make a basic choice either for God or for the world. They can't be friends with both at the same time (v. 4). The solution? Complete surrender. "Submit yourselves, then, to God. Resist the devil, and he will flee from you. Come near to God and he will come near to you. Wash your hands, you sinners, and purify your hearts, you double-minded" (vv. 7–8).

This battle for the soul is literally that. It is a struggle for the integrity of our very being, and our eternal destiny. Vacillation between God-reliance and self-reliance produces an inherently unstable life. The way to peace is complete surrender to God.

I'm grateful that God exposed the instability in my inner life by calling out my scarcity mind-set. In my heart, I was fully surrendered to God and fully committed to church multiplication. Yet my soul was divided. I experienced firsthand the tensions that James described—instability, uncertainty, relational tension. The answer for me was the answer for all who live in that netherworld of indecision: "Be transformed by the renewing of your mind."

God Leading You vs. God Leading Others

DO YOU BELIEVE
GOD CAN LEAD
OTHER PEOPLE,
INCLUDING YOUR
SPOUSE, OR IS
IT ONLY YOU TO
WHOM HE SPEAKS?

We were all there, crowded around the arrival gate at Gerald R. Ford International Airport, waiting on the last flight of the day to arrive from Chicago. It was just a short hop across Lake Michigan, but a connecting flight had been delayed in San Francisco. We were all a bit anxious, wondering if they'd arrived in time to make the last leg of their long journey from Seoul to Grand Rapids. It was nearly midnight when the arrivals board signaled that the plane had finally landed. My mom and dad were there with me, and Jan's parents, and our two boys, aged nine and eleven, along with a group of friends from Kentwood Community Church (KCC). Some were holding signs that read "Welcome Elise" and "We Love You, Ee Seul Baik."

Within a few minutes, travelers began to emerge from the Jetway. They were mostly business travelers, unmistakable by their brief cases and brisk walk. Then came a few families, looking tanned and tired, perhaps returning from winter vacations to Florida. And then came Jan, the last traveler to exit the plane, carrying our adoptive daughter, whom I was seeing for the very first time. There was applause, and laughter, and shouts of delight all around. But for me, tears. I embraced Jan and embraced Elise, and cried tears of relief and joy. The emotion was equal to what I'd experienced at the birth of my two boys, a feeling of delight and satisfaction and relief and over-whelming gladness.

That was our family's Gotcha Day, January 20, 1993, the day Elise became part of our family. And to think, I had nearly missed that joyous moment because of my stubborn reluctance to surrender to God at a point of spiritual pride.

June 1990

The hardest thing about marriage is not finding out what your spouse is really like. It's finding out what you are really like. There are aspects of yourself that don't emerge until you experience the intimacy of a marriage relationship, and this is especially true at those times when you and your spouse are in different places in your relationship with God. I found this out the hard way after twelve years of marriage and more than a decade into my pastoral career.

I had mentioned to God several times that I strongly prefer it when he reveals his will to Jan and me at the same time, preferably in the same way. That way we don't experience tension in making decisions about our future. As a bonus, I never have to face the uncomfortable question of whether it is Jan or I who is leading us deeper in following Christ.

However, God has often reminded me that he will work in the whole world and in my life in any way he sees fit. Occasionally that involves leading others to an insight or decision before leading me—or as a way of leading me. When God chose to lead my wife in a direction different from what I would have chosen, I found I had a choice to make. I could double down on my spiritual authority as a leader in the church and my perceived role as the primary decision maker in my home, or I could seriously confront this simple question: Do you believe God can lead other people, including your spouse, or is it only you to whom he speaks? While the answer may seem obvious, it is never that simple in a real-life situation. For me, that situation was the different leading experienced by Jan and me on the question of adopting a child. She was convinced it was God's will for our family. I was uncertain.

Jan and I are different in many ways that keep our relationship interesting. One of them is that I tend to follow God by looking at the long-term picture of where he is leading. I believe if you get the big picture right, the smaller steps will work themselves out. Jan tends to follow God by seeking the next simple act of obedience, keeping in step with the Spirit on smaller decisions. She believes if you consistently take the next right step, the long-term plan will work itself out. Both approaches are biblically sound, and we have the same heart to follow God wherever he leads. We just have different ways of discerning that leading. That seemingly insignificant difference widened to a chasm in August 1990 when Jan returned home from babysitting a neighbor's children.

"I think we should adopt a child," she said. "A girl." Our neighbors had two boys, just as we did, and they had two girls as well. I'd seen this coming for some time, yet as a husband I knew this was difficult ground for conversation.

Jan had had some difficulties during her pregnancies for our sons, born in 1981 and 1983. We'd accepted the doctor's advice that it was best to bear no more children. In my mind, our family was complete. I had thought Jan felt the same, and perhaps for a time she did. Yet I'd known for a while that the possibility of adoption had been stirring within her. She believed we should add a girl to our family, specifically a girl who had been born overseas. This seemed to resonate with the global vision God had placed within Jan as a young girl.

My motives for opposing the idea were less noble. I was comfortable with our family of four, which fit well with our three-bedroom house. I was concerned about the cost. I also worried about the risks of adopting an older child, having heard horror stories from friends at finding they'd taken into their home children with scarred histories and deep psychological problems.

"Well," I said, "if that's the way you feel, maybe we could look into it." I had no such desire, but I had to admit that the leading she felt seemed to be genuinely of God. I also felt a bit convicted by the fact that she'd followed me into the ministry based on my call from the Lord. Even so, I really had no wish to surrender my priorities and preferences to follow Jan's leading. Frankly, I hoped the inquiry would lead to a dead end.

I was harboring a deeper objection too, one that I became aware of only through further conversations with Jan and with my accountability partner. What if I couldn't love the child? Clearly I didn't have the same excitement about adoption that Jan had. What if I never did? Fear was beginning to overwhelm my faith, a pattern I'd seen in myself before. Fortunately, I was able to recognize that and was willing to deal with it.

I repented of my selfishness, and I soon realized God was not asking me to fake my feelings, pretending to match Jan's enthusiasm. "Don't make this matter an issue about feelings and preferences," God seemed to be saying. "Just believe that I can lead Jan as well as I can lead you." I knew that I must, as always, choose to surrender my will to God's. Only this time that will was being expressed through the desire of my wife's heart.

A few weeks after that initial conversation with Jan, I was able to tell her with more conviction that I was willing to begin the process of adoption. I was genuinely willing to proceed, and I hoped my willingness would be sacrifice enough. I still hoped I would never need to go through with an adoption.

Jan was interested in seeking a child from a South American country, and I had no objection to that—anymore than I had to the entire idea. We connected with a secular agency that specialized in adoptions from South America. A short time later, we sat for an interview with one of their specialists. The meeting was less than spectacular.

"I'm not sure it's a good idea for pastors to adopt children from overseas," she said.

"Excuse me?" Jan said. I wisely held my tongue.

The woman clarified her reasoning, saying that the burden pastors have of living in a glass house would place undue behavioral expectations on the child, which could be detrimental to her well-being.

"I think you need to get some counseling before we go any further," she added.

"You've got to be kidding me," I thought. "Who does she think she is, saying that we need counseling?

However, we reluctantly agreed because we wanted to move the process forward. Jan and I both suspected the woman's opinion reflected her own biases and experiences rather than our fitness as adoptive parents. Personally, I resented the time and money we'd have to spend to counter this woman's prejudice against the clergy. Was my resentment rooted in my spiritual Achilles' heel of insecurity? Did it rise from the fact that my surrender on the adoption issue was less than wholehearted, perhaps even passive-aggressive? If so, I wasn't yet willing to admit it, and we proceeded with counseling.

We were free to choose any licensed professional counselor, so we chose a practitioner whom we knew to be a Christian. After reviewing the results of a battery of psychological tests we'd taken, the counselor said, "You guys seem fine. I'm not even sure why you are here."

My attitude toward counseling suddenly changed. "I like this guy," I thought. "What a helpful process this is turning out to be." Our conversation proceeded comfortably for several minutes. Then, totally without warning, he dropped the bomb.

"So tell me, Wayne, why do you think it is necessary to protect Jan from your true feelings? Do you think she can't handle them?"

"What!" I said, not so much a question as an exclamation. I was stunned. I muttered some completely unconvincing explanation and retreated to my former low opinion of this counseling process. I couldn't wait for the session to be over.

Yet in the days that followed, I couldn't get the counselor's question out of my head. God seemed to be using that counseling session—one we'd attended only when forced by a non-believing adoption agent—to expose the relational walls I had constructed between Jan and me. The question exposed the extent to which my people-pleasing tendency impacted all relationships, including my relationship with my own wife. I had been willing to share my thoughts readily when I believed Jan would receive them positively, but I shared hesitantly or selectively when I was unsure how she would react. It seemed I had a filter running in the background on my feelings, like auto-correct on my computer. I quietly amended or deleted any thoughts I suspected might be hard for Jan to accept. That realization became a catalyst for change in my life and in our relationship. In the years since then, I've learned to set aside my unfounded fear of damaging our relationship, and we have come to know each other in a deeper, more honest way than we had until that time.

God used the prejudices of a secular adoption specialist to position me to learn something that would forever strengthen my marriage. Ironically, that may have been the only purpose for our interaction with that agency. A short time later, the country we had focused on chose to simplify its adoption process by reducing the number of agencies it authorized to work there. As a result, the organization we were using was no longer able to arrange adoptions from that country. That door was firmly closed.

"Oh well," I thought. "At least we tried." We had invested time and money to explore the possibility of adoption. In the process, we had learned something that would benefit our marriage for years to come. I was convinced that that was the point of the exercise, to strengthen our relationship. In my mind, the adoption question was closed. Not surprisingly, Jan saw it differently. She was convinced we should persevere. We were back to square one, but at least we were communicating more transparently with one another.

I went along with Jan's desire to continue pursuing an adoption, less grudgingly than before. In 1991 we changed agencies, this time selecting a Christian adoption organization, and began the process all over again. This agency worked primarily with Asian countries and had developed a new program to find homes for children from a conflict zone in the mountains of Myanmar. We were approved to move forward, and we received a picture of the child we would adopt, a little girl named Su Mar. She was pictured with her aunt, who was her primary caregiver since the death of Su Mar's parents. We placed her picture prominently on our refrigerator and arranged a bedroom for Su Mar in our home. In our minds, it was just a matter of time before she would come to live with us, and I have to admit that even I was warming up to the idea. I thought of Su Mar, whom we called Susan Marissa, as our little girl. We all did. But it was never to be so.

Unfortunately, our agency had been the victim of a fraud perpetrated by its in-country partner. That man, who purported to be arranging adoptions, was taking pictures of children with a parent and telling the parents that he was raising money for child sponsorships. He then sent the photos to the adoption agency, saying that the children were pictured with a relative because their parents had been killed. He was profiting from this deception. The little girl on our fridge was Su Mar pictured with her mother.

"I feel like I carried that child for nine months," Jan said, putting words to the disappointment we both felt, Jan most profoundly. We had all become attached to Su Mar and were grieved by her loss. A second door had been firmly closed, and in my mind that really did end the matter. We had tried to adopt twice, investing a good deal of time, money, and emotional energy in each attempt. I had grown from being completely closed to the idea to supporting Jan's desire to adopt to developing an emotional attachment to a child who might become our daughter. But I was through. Though she didn't say so in those words, I felt sure Jan also understood that the adoption issue had finally been put to rest.

Then one evening our family was enjoying a cookout with another family from our church. They had an adopted daughter from Korea, who had spent the first years of her life in a children's home led by an American woman known as Mama Jane. These friends knew of our adoption woes and took it upon themselves to contact Mama Jane to see if there were any little girls at the orphanage who might find a home in their pastor's family. Mama Jane claimed she had "just the right girl" for Pastor Wayne and Jan. "Were we interested?" our friends wanted to know.

When God called the young boy Samuel, it took three attempts before the old priest Eli realized that the boy was hearing the voice of God. "Speak, for your servant is listening," Samuel finally said in response (1 Sam. 3:10). Without comparing myself to the great judge of Israel, I can say that the Lord finally got through to me after three attempts. "Yes," was our resounding answer. Jan and I were now fully united in our desire to adopt. In retrospect I'm embarrassed at how long it took to reach that place of full surrender, but I was then ready to admit that God had been leading us toward this adoption all along—by speaking primarily to Jan.

Our Christian adoption agency, mortified at how they had been duped, was more than willing to partner with an adoption agency in Seoul on our behalf. By March of 1992, we got the word that we could visit Korea, and we received the available little girl's photo in June. But it wasn't until January 1993 that Jan boarded a plane bound for South Korea to pick up our daughter. It was an excruciatingly long year. Upon seeing Jan, five-year-old Ee Seul Baik, whom we would call Elise, clung to her new mom with an intensity that surprised even Mama Jane. The bond was immediate and enduring.

When Jan walked off the plane in Grand Rapids with our little girl in her arms, I admit I was still a bit nervous. I'd fully embraced the decision to adopt her, but I knew there would be difficulties. She didn't know English, and we didn't know Korean. She'd never eaten Western food, never slept in a bed, and had rarely been in a room by herself. Would my old objections come back to haunt me? No, they would not. That night we learned that smiles can bridge a language barrier. And we soon discovered that Elise was more than capable of signaling what foods she liked and those she didn't, and that she could sleep next to the bed with the boys by her side, at least for a while. Not one of my original objections to adoptions had proved to be valid in our case, especially my fear that I might not love an adoptive child. These days when Jan and I talk about Elise, Jan will quite often raise her pinkie finger as a way of saying that Daddy's little girl has him wrapped around her finger, which is quite true. I am overwhelmed by love for her.

Elise is now an amazing young woman, married to a wonderful man, and I cannot imagine our family without her in it. Mama Jane did indeed have just the right girl for Pastor Wayne and Jan. I am forever grateful to her and the many others who played a role in Elise's joining our family. I am most grateful to Jan, whose unwavering sense of God's call kept us moving in God's direction. Many of the best things in life don't come easy. They require persistence and sacrifice. And some come only when we are willing to surrender the idea that God leads us only by speaking directly to us, and accept that his most precious leading may come through the faithful witness of a another.

Surrender Requires Self-Awareness

DO NOT THINK OF YOURSELF MORE HIGHLY THAN YOU OUGHT, BUT RATHER THINK OF YOURSELF WITH SOBER JUDGMENT, IN ACCORDANCE WITH THE FAITH GOD HAS DISTRIBUTED TO EACH OF YOU.

ROMANS 12:3

Although it is tempting to think of surrender as a purely individual exercise, it is not. While surrender begins as a transaction between God and the individual, it is ultimately a communal matter. Our lives are intertwined with others' lives; therefore, our surrender to God cannot be complete until it spreads outward to envelop our relationships. Other interaction with those around us will be both an element of and a proof of our complete surrender to God.

This is what John Wesley meant when he said there is "no holiness but social holiness." This quote has been popularized a bit in recent years as a reference to social action. Some take it to mean that fully surrendered Christians must be involved in meeting the needs of others by doing things like feeding the hungry or drilling wells in developing nations. While that may be true, and John Wesley certainly was a social activist, it is not precisely what he meant by this statement. The wider context of the quote reveals that Wesley was urging believers to see their need to be in relationships with one another:

> For the religion these authors [the Mystics] would edify us in, is solitary religion. . . . He hath attained the true resignation, who hath estranged himself from all outward works, that God may work inwardly in him, without any turning toward outward things. . . .
>
> Directly opposite to this is the gospel of Christ. Solitary religion is not to be found there. "Holy solitaries" is a phrase no more consistent with the gospel than holy adulterers. The gospel of Christ knows of no religion, but social; no holiness but social holiness. "Faith working by love" is the length and breadth and depth and height of Christian perfection.[1]

Wesley was concerned that Christians would think of surrender to God as a kind of withdrawal into the self. Having achieved an inner purity of intention, a perfect love for God, they would forget about the second part of the Great Commandment—to love others. That's not the gospel, Wesley asserted. It is not possible to be a Christian all by yourself. The surrendered life must be expressed in our relationships. Otherwise, it is not surrender at all.

That's essentially what I discovered in my offering plate moment in 1990 and the events that followed. I had conceived of my surrender to God as a purely individual thing. This was between God and me. He called me into ministry, and I sorted through my inner life to process that call. Then I responded. I was delighted Jan wanted to join *me* on *my* journey, but I was following the leading God had revealed to me. That made it confusing when she sensed God was leading *us* to adopt a child, something about which I had no direction from the Lord. How could God lead Jan in a direction he hadn't led me? What if we couldn't resolve the matter? Why should I sacrifice my needs and desires for something God hadn't revealed to me? I was asking questions that get at the social aspect of surrender. In the end, I discovered others can prompt our surrender to God and our surrender—or unwillingness to surrender—can have a deep impact on others as well. Relationships are the sandbox in which surrender is played out. There is no holiness but social holiness.

We see the concept of social, or relational, surrender in Romans 12. Paul began the chapter with a call to surrender ("offer your bodies as a living sacrifice," v. 1) and continued with a call to self-assessment ("think of yourself with sober judgment," v. 3). He moved finally to a call to social action ("Be devoted to one another in love," v. 10). The word *for* in verse 3 tells us that the calls to self-assessment and social action are related to the call to surrender. Surrendered persons will have a sober—in this case meaning level-headed and accurate— opinion of themselves. As a result, they will interact with others based on love, not self-interest or, for that matter, self-abasement. So as we fill out our picture of the surrendered life, it looks something like this. Surrender leads to a greater self-awareness, and that results in loving action toward others. We are not lone rangers, each doing his or her own thing for God. We are one part of a relational system, a body, and we know our place in it.

Often, thinking on the subject of surrender jumps over that middle part, self-awareness. That's an easy mistake to make since Jesus' own teaching seemed to focus on the first and third elements: love of God and love of others. Yet the idea of self-knowledge is implicit in Jesus' teaching on this very point. When asked which is the greatest commandment, Jesus replied, "'Love the Lord your God with all your heart and with all your soul and with all your mind.' This is the first and greatest commandment. And the second is like it: 'Love your neighbor as yourself'" (Matt. 22:37–40). Love for others must accompany love for God, and that love is moderated by self-knowledge. This echoes Jesus's Golden Rule, "Do to others as you would have them do to you" (Luke 6:31). Right treatment of others depends on a right assessment of ourselves. We can't have one without the other. Self-awareness is vital to the surrendered life.

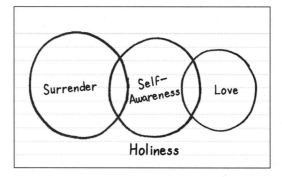

Let's take a closer look at self-awareness. If our transformation into the likeness of Christ depends on being self-aware, what can we learn from Scripture and experience about cultivating this "sober judgment" of ourselves?

Principles for Self-Examination

Our capacity to see ourselves clearly plays a vital role in our transformation. Yet self-assessment is a tricky thing. One danger is that we spend so much time thinking about ourselves, we become entirely self-focused. It's possible to run from relationship to relationship, self-help book to online survey, and even from church to church continually asking the question "How am I doing?" Self-examination can lead to self-absorption.

Too little self-inquiry is just as dangerous. I was blindsided when the counselor confronted my unwillingness to share my true feelings about adoption with Jan. My lack of self-awareness was hindering my ability to extend my surrender to God into my relationships. I was unwilling to be completely open and honest with others, even my own wife, and I was unaware that I was doing so. So when it comes to self-assessment, the twin dangers are that we will either overthink it or underthink it. Clearly we need balance when examining ourselves. Here are several principles that can help achieve that balance.

Self-Assessment Should Lead beyond the Self

Thinking about yourself must be joined with getting beyond yourself. Immediately after giving the two imperatives for self-knowledge in Romans 12 ("think of yourself," v. 3), Paul launched into a description of our life together (vv. 4–8). He compared us to parts of a body, stressing that we each have a part to play. To play that role, we must be fully aware of both our place and the place of others. We have a common life. "Each member belongs to all the others" (v. 5). So the purpose of self-assessment is not to either build up or tear down the self. It is to find one's own place in the web of relationships within the body of Christ. You can't discover that by looking only at yourself. The process of self-discovery must have another, greater object: the discovery of others.

The brilliance of John Wesley's approach to spiritual formation lies not only in his optimistic view of grace. Wesley did
indeed believe in the power of God to transform the lives of
those who surrendered to him. Yet Wesley knew internal
surrender was not enough. His true genius was in gathering
people into groups that would sustain their expectation and
devotion, the two elements of our Grace Grid. From societies
(large groups) to classes (small groups) to bands (accountability
groups) to select bands (mentoring groups) and even penitent
bands (recovery groups), the corporate nature of early Method-
ism ensured that believers would not retreat into isolationism
or stray into individualism. They pursued the surrendered life
together.

Self-Assessment Examines the Inner Life

As we've already seen, the aspects of personhood we are
referring to as the soul—that is emotions, mind, and volition—
are vital for complete surrender. In his command to understand
ourselves, Paul instructed us to engage these very elements of
our being. We must delve into the inner life, something many
people avoid doing. The Greek word translated as *think* is used
multiple times in verse 3, emphasizing by sheer repetition the
idea that we must deal seriously with the inner life. Simply
spending time in personal reflection is a good place to begin.
Beyond that, it is useful to understand the soulish elements of
our nature in their own right.

The concept of *emotional intelligence*—the capacity to
accurately recognize emotions in oneself and others and to use
that knowledge in decision-making and social relationships—
was coined by psychologist Daniel Goleman.[2] The fact that
Goleman's book by the same name became an instant best
seller when it appeared in 1995 and has been translated into
forty languages may be a clue to the fact that many people
lack insight into their own feelings. To accurately assess

yourself, it's vital to gain insight into the basic ways in which you think, experience emotions, and make decisions. Though not definitive tools, instruments such as the DiSC assessment, Myers-Briggs Type Indicator, and StrengthsFinder can be useful for gaining insight into your own emotional and intellectual wiring. The understanding gained from these tools leads almost immediately to a desire to understand the thought patterns of family members, friends, and coworkers. When you see your own soul patterns clearly, you are much better able to understand the ways others think and react.

Self-Awareness Produces Gifts Awareness

Though often confused, personal strengths are not the same as spiritual gifts. The former are gifts of God's common grace, given to us at birth. Some of us are more decisive while others more reflective, some introverted and others fueled by social interaction. Paul pushed us to think beyond those categories to the particular graces we have received through the Holy Spirit. These are gifts that go beyond our natural abilities to do things such as prophesying, serving, teaching, encouragement, or generosity (vv. 6–8). The point of self-assessment is not simply to know the things you're particularly good at, but to see the unique contribution you make to the body of Christ. A number of tools are available for assessing spiritual giftedness, just as there are for gaining insight into temperament. These tools are of some value, but remember that spiritual gifts go beyond personal preferences or natural abilities. They are gifts from God, not natural talents or inclinations. Prayer, personal reflection, and the counsel of others may prove more useful in assessing your spiritual gifts.

Self-Assessment Can Stray High or Low

Paul specifically warned of two dangers in the pursuit of self-knowledge. One is thinking of ourselves more highly than we ought to think (v. 3). Sometimes this over-estimation comes from too little self-examination. That was my experience in 1990. I simply wasn't aware of some dynamics of my inner life because I'd not given the subject enough thought. An inflated sense of self also can result from thinking too much about oneself, or perhaps thinking in the wrong ways. All of us tend to make ourselves the hero of our own story. We can develop a sort of confirmation bias, wrongly interpreting nearly everything that happens in life as proof that we're right and others are wrong, or that we're somehow more worthy.

A second danger in assessing the self is that we will under-value ourselves and our role in the community. Paul put his finger on this when he wrote that we should think of ourselves "in accordance with the faith God has distributed to each of you" (v. 3). It isn't that we want to devalue ourselves, but that we want an accurate assessment. That will come from looking not at our own thoughts only nor even through the lens of others, but from God's perspective. We are seeking to gain a sober view of ourselves, one that doesn't stagger into the ditch on either side of the road.

Interestingly, Paul warned about this same over- or under-estimation of self in 1 Corinthians 12, another passage that deals with giftedness. The thought that "I do not belong" (v. 15) is classic underestimation, and the assessment that "I don't need you" (v. 21) places too much value on oneself. In fact, we all need each other. The point of self-assessment is to figure out your role with others. It should never result in either isolating the self or rejecting others. Beware of any self-assessment process that leads to those conclusions.

Community Aids Self-Awareness

Being in relationships with others helps you arrive at and maintain a realistic perspective about yourself. You may have seen a warning on the back of some trucks to alert other motorists of the truck driver's blind spot. The sign reads, "If you can't see my mirrors, I can't see you." We all have blind spots in our thinking about ourselves. Other people can serve as the mirrors that reflect reality to us. Spouses and parents are good examples. Both are often willing to give feedback, sometimes uninvited, that adjusts our perspective on ourselves. When given lovingly, that advice is an invaluable source of information about ourselves. Wesley was right: there is no substitute for relationships in the spiritual life. Other people help us work out surrender in the real world. And we help them as well.

One aspect of this social spirituality that is often missing in the current expression of the church in the West, which so heavily emphasizes the role of individual, is the concept of *collective conscience.* Historically, the church has recognized that God's leading of the community is just as important for an individual as is his or her own conscience. The Jerusalem Council, reported in Acts 15, shows this principle in action. While there are a number of issues about which we exercise personal conscience, there are other issues to which the church speaks collectively. In Acts 15, the body concluded that individuals were free to follow their conscience on the question of circumcision, but that everyone should avoid sexual immorality and certain other practices (Acts 15:19–20). While I personally may not have a clear direction from the Lord on some difficult doctrinal issues or on certain aspects of the Christian lifestyle, I accept the collective conscience of the church on these matters. I allow myself to be led by God's leading of the body. This is another aspect of social holiness.

The Well-Differentiated Person

Paul's idea that we must think of ourselves with sober judgment in order to fully surrender to God is well-illustrated by the work of Edwin Friedman, a rabbi and family therapist who has written on the subject of leadership. Specifically, Friedman's concept of the "well-differentiated leader" may help us dig deeper into Paul's concept of self-knowledge as a key to surrender. In his book *A Failure of Nerve: Leadership in the Age of the Quick Fix*, Friedman describes well-differentiated leaders versus those who draw their concept of self from the organization, the praise of others, or the situation around them. Well-differentiated leaders possess:

- the capacity to separate oneself from surrounding emotional processes,
- the capacity to obtain clarity about one's principles and vision,
- the willingness to be exposed and be vulnerable,
- the persistence to face inertial resistance,
- the self-regulation of emotions in the face of reactive sabotage.[3]

Self-knowledge and self-control are critical traits of a well-differentiated leader, or person.

You can probably name some leaders who do not possess these traits. They often become slaves to consensus because they are unable to differentiate the success of the organization from their own well-being, or the good opinion of others from their own concept of self. They don't see themselves clearly, so they are unable to function effectively. Well-differentiated leaders, on the other hand, are able to step outside their context emotionally and make what Paul would call a "sober judgment" of themselves and their situation. They understand who they are apart from their constituents, the voters, parishioners, customers, and so on. As a result, they are able to hold positions or take risks that may be upsetting to others. In other words, they are able to lead.

Let's apply that idea to the concept of surrender. When our concept of ourselves is drawn primarily from others, we are unable to surrender fully to God because we're always worried about what others think of us. However, when we are able to step outside ourselves and see who we are from God's perspective and see others as they truly are, we are free to use the gifts God has given us without being paralyzed by the opinions of others. In other words, we're free to live out the surrender we have made to God.

The ABCs of Surrender

We can summarize the ABCs of surrender with three ideas: awareness, becoming, and connecting. When we are self-aware, we are enabled to become the persons God intends us to be. As we do, our connection with others will grow.

Awareness

This process begins with self-awareness, or thinking of ourselves with "sober judgment," as Paul put it. We must engage with our inner life of mind, emotions, and intentions, seeing ourselves according to the "faith God has distributed" to us. I've already mentioned some basic tools for gaining insight into the way we think. There are others that specifically integrate aspects of our spiritual life. One is the book *S.H.A.P.E.: Finding and Fulfilling Your Unique Purpose for Life* by Erik Rees. Based on Rick Warren's *The Purpose-Driven Life, S.H.A.P.E.* guides readers to understand their purpose through spiritual gifts, heart, abilities, personal style, and experiences. The Grip-Birkman assessment aims to help people find and fulfill their role in the body by examining three primary questions: Where am I strong? Where am I weak? What do I need?

Regardless of the process, self-awareness is a necessary component of surrender. Self-awareness has been so instrumental in my development for ministry and in the development of Kentwood Community Church during its formative years that when I presided over Wesley Seminary at Indiana Wesleyan University, I ensured that one of the six spiritual formation units in the MDiv program focused on self-awareness. I'm convinced we cannot be fully effective in ministry to others without first seeing ourselves clearly.

Becoming

A proper self-understanding will lead us deeper into surrender. We see this in the progression of thought in Romans 12, where knowing ourselves leads to serving others. Knowing ourselves helps us to be ourselves in the truest sense, the selves we were created to be. When we have self-knowledge, we are able to self-regulate our behavior. Think of the numerous biblical references to self-control, particularly Galatians 5:22–23, where it is named as a fruit of the Spirit along with qualities such as love, joy, kindness, and gentleness. We all know the danger and frustration of trying to be something we are not. We're never successful at it for long, and when we are able to feign the fruit we do not possess, we feel the added stress of being hypocritical. But where there is self-knowledge, self-control is possible. We understand who we are and who we wish to be, and we make progress in that direction. As Paul wrote, "Each one should test their own actions. Then they can take pride in themselves alone, without comparing themselves to someone else" (Gal. 6:4).

Connecting

When we become self-aware—but not self-absorbed—we are freer to connect with others. This is the point of Paul's thinking in Romans 12:3–8. Once you discover who you are in the context of deep relationships, you will be free to become connected, but not enmeshed, with others. This is the well-differentiated person. As I discovered during the process of adopting a child, my challenge in being a married person was not simply to get to know my wife and her desires. I fully understood what she wanted. The real challenge was in coming to grips with who I was. I didn't fully understand my own motivations at the time; therefore, I was unable to be fully unified with Jan. When I came to see myself clearly, I was able to connect with my wife at a level of emotional and spiritual intimacy we hadn't yet experienced.

In each of these ABCs—awareness, becoming, connecting— there is a danger of being false. It's possible to feign self-awareness while hiding areas of our emotional or intellectual lives from others and perhaps even from ourselves. In the area of becoming, we can pretend a level of self-mastery we have not attained. This hypocrisy creates a compartmentalized or hypocritical life. And at the level of connection, it is possible to enter connections with others that seem transparent and collaborative on the surface but which really serve an ego need. We want to be affirmed or needed, so we surrender a measure of our autonomy to others. Faking any one of the ABCs is dangerous, but perhaps more so in the area of connecting. A self-aware person is able to be emotionally available. Those without self-awareness are likely to become enmeshed in the emotional needs or wants of others, losing themselves in the process. The ABCs must work together.

I'm convinced that when the ABCs work together, a rhythm of self-awareness develops. Solitude and reflection lead to self-awareness. That new self-awareness leads to greater self-control, both in a negative and positive sense. We are better able to avoid destructive behaviors and to engage in the constructive role God has created for us. That leads to deeper connection with others, which will inevitably be tested by people trying to impose on us their ideas of who we should be. We will face the temptation to please others rather than loving people and pleasing God. That discomfort will drive us back to seeking renewed self-understanding, and the cycle begins again.

Beginning with my offering plate moment in 1990, I have seen this cycle played out dozens of times in my own life and ministry. The desire to please people is a constant temptation in ministry. That makes it vital to have a sober judgment of ourselves, understanding who God has made us to be and what our role is with others. That's true for any Christian, of course, not just for leaders. As I reflect on my offering plate moment, I see that it began when I was able to set aside my initial preference and explore the possibility of adoption. However, I still did not have an accurate self-awareness, and that led to a false way of being—seeming to be open to adoption when I harbored deep reservations. I'm grateful for the probing question of a counselor who was able to penetrate that superficial agreement and force me to see myself clearly. That moment was the beginning of a self-discovery that took my surrender to God to an even deeper level, and brought me into closer connection with Jan than ever before. Right treatment of others depends on a right assessment of ourselves. Self-awareness is vital to the surrendered life.

Submission vs. Self-Preservation

MY MOMENT OF
SURRENDER LED
TO GREATER
DEPENDENCE
UPON GOD.

December 1999
The term Y2K has long since passed from our cultural consciousness, but in December of 1999, it was a hot topic. For months, tension had been building around this issue, which involved a glitch in the computer systems we all rely on. Computers then routinely reported the date in a six-digit format, two digits each for month, day, and year. The problem was that with the turn of the century on January 1, 2000, computers

would be unable to distinguish dates in the new century from those of the previous one. What would happen? Would computers reading the date as January 1900 issue pension checks for retirees born in the 1920s? Would airline computers recognize flights that appeared to have taken place one hundred years ago? Would stoplights work? Would mail be delivered? Would life as we knew it grind to a halt?

None of those things occurred, of course, and the new millennium arrived without a hitch. But in 1999, few people knew what would happen. All we knew was a computer bug that had been allowed to exist for decades had suddenly become an urgent problem that threatened everyone's well-being.

It is tempting to look back with amusement on the ways some of us succumbed to the hysteria of that time, filling our basements with canned goods and bottled water. But I didn't, because, as the "millennium bug" swept the nation, I was dealing with a crisis of another kind. A problem I had ignored far too long was about to erupt in my life and ministry. Like a nervous computer technician, I ushered in the year 2000 filled with trepidation about the future. But unlike those dealing with the Y2K problem, I had a secret option available to me. I could run away.

Lunch with my friend and mentor Jerry DeRuiter was always a pleasure. A longtime member of Kentwood Community Church (KCC), Jerry had become a key leader in the congregation and a trusted personal advisor. Given that he was a former mayor of Kentwood and a former county commissioner, I especially valued Jerry's keen insight on matters of governance. He served as the vice-chairperson of the KCC board making him the lay leader of the congregation. KCC had a strong, well-organized board that functioned well in its oversight role, thanks in part to Jerry's wisdom. While some church boards have a tendency to micromanage, diving down into administrative or operations decisions that are best left to the pastor and staff, the KCC board avoided that. The board met quarterly and focused on the higher-level matters of clarifying the mission, setting boundaries, and providing accountability to the lead pastor. The board exercised oversight; the staff operated the church. I was grateful to have a vice-chairperson who understood that distinction. We met on a cloudy December day at Arnie's, a family-style restaurant on the west side of Kentwood.

"So what can I do for you?" I asked after we'd placed our order. Jerry had asked for the meeting, and I assumed he wanted to discuss something about the church budget. At least I hoped that's all it was. A quarterly board meeting was scheduled for the next month.

"I'm going to level with you, Wayne," he said, which was Jerry's style: come right to the point. "The staff situation is creating real conflict in the church. People are starting to take sides in a way that could do permanent damage. We need a resolution, and we need it now."

The "staff situation" he referred to was a simmering conflict with a senior staff member, a conflict I had been avoiding. Factions were forming among the staff and the congregation. For a variety of reasons, I'd chosen to ignore this issue over the years, thus allowing a wrongly positioned leader to become entrenched in a key role. My inaction allowed the conflict to spread to the point of including the staff, board members, and even the congregation. The board was well aware of these dynamics, as Jerry's next statement demonstrated.

"At next month's meeting, the board is going to ask two questions," Jerry said. "What qualities do we need in a senior pastor to lead this church into the future? And does Wayne Schmidt have those qualities?"

The words were not intended as a threat, and I know they were as painful for Jerry to say as they were for me to hear. He simply wanted me to understand that the board intended to fulfill its mandate to govern the church's ministry. If I were unwilling or unable to lead the church, the board would have to initiate a change. Jerry also let me know that if the board determined I was capable of providing the necessary leadership going forward, they would join me in asking those same questions concerning each member of the pastoral staff and would hold me accountable to act on our findings. Like the Y2K problem, the latent conflict on our team had become too urgent to ignore.

I should have been better prepared for the conflict. I certainly saw it coming, and I had the training to deal with it. Several years earlier, I had completed a doctorate in ministry and the most impacting class in the program was titled "Power, Change, and Conflict Management." My doctoral project focused on leading change. I had learned about the sources of conflict and how the solutions for any conflict resolution must fit the source. I had discovered my own preferred method for handling conflict, which was avoidance, and how to counter my preference when it was not appropriate or productive in resolving conflict. I also had plenty of experience in putting what I'd learned into action. Leading KCC from its inception through multiple building programs and growth to some twenty-five hundred attendees had brought its share of controversy and conflict.

Though my head was ready for the challenge, my heart was not. I had not fully grieved the death of my father, who had passed away while I was still in my thirties. Also, I was conflict weary. Some of our decisions and strategies as a local church had created tension in valued relationships with our denomination. That weighed heavily on me because of my love for the Wesleyan movement. I had said good-bye to some close friends and prayer partners, who indicated they were leaving KCC because they could not share our vision. I had no heart for battle so it seemed easier to ignore the building tensions.

In hindsight I can also see that spiritual warfare may have played a part in this conflict. For instance, in 1999 a couple of newlyweds named Kyle and Petra Ray started attending KCC. I couldn't have known then that God would call Kyle, a successful engineer, into vocational ministry, or that God would work through his outreach gifts to help our church become more diverse and to more fully reflect our community, or that God would call him to be the next lead pastor of KCC a decade later. Perhaps the enemy was creating a hostile environment to disrupt these possibilities before they could develop.

While I knew that others bore the responsibility for the division then taking place within the church, I also knew that I was complicit due to my unwillingness to face and resolve matters much earlier. I had withdrawn into my default style of dealing with conflict: avoidance. That left me, after twenty years at KCC, facing a deeply rooted conflict that had been several years in the making, and it threatened to end my leadership at the church I'd help to found. Further, I still believed I was called to the ministry of KCC for life.

The month or so between my meeting with Jerry and the January board meeting seemed to drag on forever, despite the welcome relief of the Christmas celebration. I felt as if I were being roasted over a spit, the anxiety burning within me a little more each day. Finally the board retreat came, a day-long meeting held at a local conference facility. The board identified its priorities for the lead pastor, then compared that list to my capabilities. Like a Y2K doomsayer, I had spent the month imagining the worst. I feared the board would conclude I wasn't the leader the church needed, that I would be, in effect, fired. But to my great relief, the board saw a strong correlation between the church's need and my capacity. They gave me a unanimous vote of confidence.

That relief was short-lived. At the same meeting, the board concluded, and I agreed, that certain key staff members were no longer willing or able to fulfill their intended roles. The next step would be for me to have the hard conversations that would deliver that news, along with a statement of my resolve and the board's. I would have to confront, demote, or remove staff members who had been friends and were also influential in our congregation. I knew full well what the result would be. Some would dispute these conclusions. They had already put into place subtle but sophisticated defense mechanisms and recruited supporters to their defense. Already I was facing attacks on my leadership, some of which were very personal. That would only escalate as we moved forward with our plan. The conflict that I had avoided for so long was about to erupt in full force, and there was simply no place to hide.

A few days after the board retreat, I stayed late at the office, brooding about the impending storm. If the two most common responses to a conflict are fight and flight, I knew I was in no mood for a fight. Flight seemed like the only option. After years of dealing with routine conflicts that every pastor faces, the conflicts and criticism unique to church planting, and the heart-rending conflicts that had come along with asking hard questions and pushing boundaries within my denomination, I was bone weary. I felt empty, exhausted, and done. In an act of prayer, and perhaps a sign of my total emptiness, I lay face down on the floor and began to weep.

"Let me go, Lord," I cried. "I can't do this anymore, and I don't want to. I can't face one more complaint or criticism or attack. Release me. Release me." A few days earlier, I had been terrified at the thought that the church board might find me unfit to lead and let me go. Now I was begging God to be absolved of the call I had thought would last for my lifetime. Such was the depth of hopelessness about this situation.

There have been a few occasions in my life when God spoke clearly, directly, and unmistakably to me. This was one of them. In response to my plea, God said: "Wayne, you contributed to this mess, and you need to invest the remnant of credibility to clean it up. Take courage. It's a big mess, and you will have to persevere. If you do, by the church's twenty-fifth anniversary, it will be fully healthy and externally focused once again." Though his voice was not audible, that message was as clear to me as the words on this page.

I wish that unmistakable communication had been enough to rouse my spirits, but, like Elijah, whining to the Lord in 1 Kings 19, I had not yet exhausted my self-pity. I dared to press the argument further. "Then what?" I asked. "What if I stick it out for five more years? Will I be able to stay and benefit from the good days that follow, or will that be my time to move on?"

Once again, I clearly sensed God communicating to me. "That's for me to know, not you. Your work will be the same for the next five years no matter what happens when that time is done."

I begged God to release me from my responsibility so I could leave the problem behind. God said no. He clearly indicated that over the coming years I'd be expected (and empowered) to clean up the problems I'd allowed to grow through my failure to lead. I could not avoid them further by running away now.

As I lay on the floor wiping my tears, I'm sad to say that this thought came to mind. At that moment, no one else knew about this call from God to stay at KCC and work through difficult issues over multiple years. It occurred to me that I could easily resign my position and spiritualize the rationale for running away. I could report that, after twenty years, God had released me to serve elsewhere. My time at KCC had come to an end, and God was moving me on. I would appear to be humble, obedient, and sensitive to the Holy Spirit. People would admire me for taking what I could present as a step of faith. Only I would know it was actually blatant disregard for God's revealed will. Even so, the idea was tempting.

Yet, even as I pondered that alternative, I knew an offering plate moment was upon me. As painful as it would be to speak difficult truths, and live them, I had to do so. I knew that I disliked the disapproval of others, but I also knew that I could not live with the disapproval of God. Hearing his command but rejecting it, then spinning my rejection to appear as obedience, would be ruinous for me spiritually. Choosing to please God would mean choosing not to please others, even myself. I understood that. And I surrendered to the right choice, though it was the more painful one.

In the days that followed, I proceeded with the hard work of holding difficult conversations, and initiating change. The next years were trying in many ways. There were good times, yes, as church health and outreach increased, but there were also losses. Many people asked questions about the actions we took, and some were dissatisfied with the answers. They chose to leave. The church entered a season of pruning.

Personally, my moment of surrender led to greater dependence upon God. I learned that engaging conflict early greatly increases the probability of a positive outcome. I developed skill in handling crucial conversations, which would serve me well and, more important, serve God well in the years to come. Engaging in those conversations was difficult at first, and I was motivated more by external accountability than by internal drive. Eventually, however, I was able to experience enough satisfaction from doing what's best for God's people that I began to proactively initiate conflict resolution. I still dislike it, but I value it and find contentment in doing it when needed.

One of the things that makes surrender so tortuous is our inability to predict its outcome. Sometimes surrendering to God means that it's time to go, to uproot from a position of comfort and step into a nomadic spiritual adventure. At other times, surrender means that it's time to stay, to persevere in present difficulties, rejecting the allure of easy escapism. My call to ministry was a call to step into the unknown, and I embraced the uncertainty. My call to stay at KCC was a call to remain in the known, to return to a field of difficult labor and tackle even harder challenges than before. In this case, I embraced the certainty, the certainty of painful conflict in valued relationships. Over a lifetime of ministry, I've found that both types of surrender are equally necessary and equally satisfying.

Surrender Deepens Relationships

LOVE MUST BE
SINCERE. HATE WHAT
IS EVIL; CLING TO
WHAT IS GOOD. BE
DEVOTED TO ONE
ANOTHER IN LOVE.
HONOR ONE ANOTHER
ABOVE YOURSELVES.

ROMANS 12:9–10

If there is no holiness but social holiness, then our surrender to God must not merely include but also impact our relationships with others. As we are changed through our surrender to God, that surrender changes the way we relate to others. We become more transparent and more honest, and we relate to others in a deeper way than before. This was my discovery after years of reflecting on my offering plate moment of 1999. That decision was the most emotionally wrenching moment I had experienced in ministry. As is often the case with events of that magnitude, I continued to process and learn from it for years afterward. Through years of theological reflection, I came to see two things clearly. First, my reluctance to engage fully in certain relationships was a factor that allowed the conflict to develop. Had I been more willing to be more honest more quickly, the conflict would likely have been smaller and less painful to resolve. Second, as I surrendered more fully to God, my relationships with others took on new depth. Though I had not been purposefully insincere in the past, having embraced God's call to remain at Kentwood Community Church (KCC), my relationships with staff members, board members, and others were marked by greater transparency on my part and a greater willingness to be straightforward, even when doing so uncovered a latent conflict.

We see this pattern in Paul's teaching in Romans 12. Surrender leads to an accurate self-assessment and a willingness to embrace community (vv. 3–8). In other words, we see ourselves more clearly, and we are willing to invest in others more fully. That change of heart in turn changes the way we relate to others on a practical level. This is the focus of verses 9 through 20, beginning with the simple statement, "Love must be sincere" (v. 9). Our guarded way of presenting ourselves to others, usually based on a desire to preserve our self-image or to avoid displeasing others, gives way to openness. It is not that we become brutally honest but that we are lovingly sincere. We do not hide, and we do not allow others to hide either. Our surrender to God deepens and transforms our relationships.

What characterizes this new, deeper level of relationship? Following Paul's thought in verses 9 and 10, we can identify four hallmarks of relational depth: integrity, sincerity, honesty, and priority.

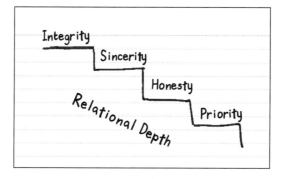

Integrity

The first hallmark of relational depth is integrity. More than a hallmark or characteristic, integrity is the foundation of loving relationships. If we are to have the kind of relationships Paul described in Romans 12:10–17, we must become whole persons. We are not naturally inclined to deep relationships beyond family and perhaps a very few close friends. And we are not, by nature, trustworthy enough for others to engage us at a deeper level. Recall the list of relational values Paul mentioned in this passage: honoring others above ourselves, sharing and practicing hospitality, blessing those who persecute us, associating with people who are not in a position to benefit us, and foregoing revenge. Presumably, this is just a sample of the kind of behavior Paul was advocating. He nearly quoted this list verbatim from Christ's Sermon on the Mount (Matt. 5–7). This kind of behavior is an inversion of the natural (fallen) order of relationships. It is simply not the way we usually relate to others. Left to our own devices, we are self-serving and self-protecting. We need a change of heart in order to be open with others, and that results from our surrender to God (Rom. 12:1), the transformation of our minds (v. 2), and our fearless self-examination (v. 3).

It is important to remember that integrity—the integration of our whole self with the heart of God—is God's work. Our part is surrender to the Spirit's filling and obedience to the Spirit's promptings. It is God who makes the change in our hearts. Accountability cannot produce this; it can only reinforce it. Transformation begins not on the outside but on the inside, with a heart fully surrendered to God. He then works it out through our mind and body, into our relationships with those around us. We can't do this alone.

Sometimes the reasons we don't surrender at this deep level, and therefore do not love others in deeper ways, are buried far down inside the soul. In my own case, my pattern of insecurity that manifested itself in a desire to please others fueled my avoidance of conflict. It wasn't that I chose to be insincere or felt competitive or spiteful toward others. My block to deeper relationships was much more subtle than that. I just didn't want to offend others. Few of us see our desire to avoid pain as something that will damage our relationships; yet, in my case, that's what happened. I had to surrender my desire for self-protection before I could love others at the level required by Romans 12.

To go deeper in any relationship, whether with God, in a marriage, or in any other context, we must move to a deeper place in our own heart. We can love others only as fully as we love God and as deeply as we know ourselves. Falseness in any form is a relationship killer. When we are false with God (or try to be, no one can truly hide from God), we do not surrender ourselves at a deep level. When we refuse to engage in self-examination, glossing over our faults, insecurities, and needs, we cannot be fully open with others. And, of course, any form of falseness with others breaks trust, which halts relationships in their tracks.

We can see this pattern clearly in marriage or other romantic attachments. When we are not fully self-aware, we become insecure. That often manifests itself in jealousy or controlling behaviors. Those behaviors undermine trust, which deepens our insecurity, and the cycle continues. So our capacity to give and receive love is directly tied to our level of surrender—first to God, then to another. Integrity is the foundation of deep relationships.

Sincerity

The second hallmark of relational depth is sincerity. Paul listed this first, and its importance cannot be overstated: "Love must be sincere" (v. 9). Insincerity undermines relationships. Sincerity builds them. Paul's thought is expressed in the original language without a verb. It comes out something like an exclamation: love sincere! The opposite of this kind of love is hypocrisy. Sincere love dispenses with role-playing. It rises from integrity. Those who are sincere do not try to present themselves as something they are not. They do not misrepresent their motives. They are exactly what they appear to be.

Those who deal falsely in relationships always have a hidden motive. Their dealings with others are tainted by self-interest. This was at the root of my initial unwillingness to confront the latent conflict at KCC. Though I might have spiritualized my rationale, thinking that I was sparing the feelings of others or protecting the church in some way, the real problem was my hidden motive of self-protection. Interestingly, this lack of sincerity was far more visible to others than I knew. By the time I was willing to admit what was happening, the entire board and many others in the church were aware of it. Others often see us more clearly than we see ourselves.

Insincere love often manifests itself in a form of role-playing or hypocrisy. We may play the concerned neighbor, the devoted spouse, or the loyal friend, but harbor some second motive such as a desire for control or gratification or inside information.

When that lack of sincerity is exposed, as it inevitably is, trust is destroyed and the relationship suffers. Sometimes the damage is irreparable. If you have been transformed by the grace of God and if you are fully self-aware, you will be able to set aside such secondary motives and love sincerely. Your relationships will be characterized by openness, genuineness, and heartfelt concern without a whiff of hypocrisy. Can you imagine the effect that might have on your family relationships, your church, or community?

Honesty

Honesty is the third hallmark of relational depth. When we act from a place of integrity and approach others with sincere motives, we will have the freedom to be honest with ourselves and with them. We will be able to speak the truth in love.

It is a mistake to think of sincere love as either blindness to faults or as a longsuffering tolerance of evil. True love may be kind, but it is not blind. Paul made that clear in his next description of loving relationships: "Hate what is evil; cling to what is good" (v. 9). The word *hate* might also be translated as *abhor*. It means to shrink back from or to flee from. We hear this same urgency in Paul's commands to "flee from sexual immorality" (1 Cor. 6:18) and "flee the evil desires of youth and pursue righteousness, faith, love and peace" (2 Tim. 2:22). If someone is in danger, the loving thing to do is to yell, "Run for your life!" There is no need to pussyfoot around the truth. When you love someone sincerely, you will be more concerned for that person's well-being than for their feelings or yours. This is not a license to be caustic or rude. Beware of the desire to gloat or to inflict insult, which can masquerade as a desire for truth. That hidden motive signals a need for deeper surrender and fuller self-awareness.

The second half of Paul's command in Romans 12:9 is "cling to what is good." The word *cling* is based on the same Greek root as the word for glue. It can be used for any type of bond, physical, emotional, or spiritual. Paul elsewhere used the Greek word to describe sexual relations (1 Cor. 6:16) and our union with Christ (v. 17). This is a strong term, and it indicates a strong bond.

When I think of the word *cling*, I picture the plastic wrap used to cover food containers, usually a dish of leftovers. I recall a television ad for a brand of plastic wrap that compared it with a cheaper brand. Both seemed to cling well while the dishes were upright, but the real test was when they were inverted. The bargain brand failed to cling, spilling the contents of the dish onto the floor. In life, the test of our ability to cling to what is good comes not when things are going well but when life turns upside down. When it is not rewarding to do the right thing, do we still cling to what is good?

To hate what is evil and cling to what is good requires discernment. In other words, it means we have to make judgments about what is evil and what is good. In the present, we seem increasingly unwilling to do that. We might say about ourselves or others, "A loving God wouldn't judge me (or them)," or, "If you love me, you won't judge me." Such statements reveal a lack of sincerity rather than a depth of love. We fail to make right judgments when motivated by a desire to protect self or avoid conflict. Love is not blind. It makes a distinction between evil and good, running from one and clinging to the other. This loving discernment and the courage to make such honest judgments are needed in our culture like never before. Remember, however, this judgment is moderated by sincerity. We are motivated not by our need to be right, to control others, or to prove biblical truth, as if that were necessary. We deal with individuals openly and honestly only because we have their good and the good of others at heart.

Priority

The fourth hallmark of relational depth is priority. Paul urged us to "be devoted to one another in love" and to "honor one another above yourselves" (Rom. 12:10). This language of devotion and honor speaks to priority. It is not possible to have deep relationships without striving toward that goal. Relationships are simply too much work to happen on their own. They must be cultivated over time, and that requires intentionality.

The Greek term *philostorgas,* which is translated here as "devoted," is a combination of two other terms, both meaning love. *Philos* is the Greek word meaning friendship, and *storge* is a word meaning natural love of family. This is not a love based on attractiveness or desirability, because you can't choose your relatives! It is a bond that goes deeper than mere preference or emotion. Paul's use of this unique term strongly counters the notion of love that is predominant in our culture—that love is a feeling. While it is certainly a matter of the heart, love involves volition. We choose to love. Even within the church, we often establish and pursue fellowship relationships based on affinity or feelings. We reach out to those who are like us or from whom we derive good feelings. This is not the love Paul described in Romans 12, which is a hallmark of our relational depth.

A paraphrase of the first statement in verse 10 might read something like this: "Make it a priority to love each other, loving people like part of the family." Paul defined this particular concept of love more explicitly in 1 Thessalonians 4:9, saying, "Now about your love for one another we do not need to write to you, for you yourselves have been taught by God to love each other." Our love for each other is patterned on the love God has shown for us in sacrificially giving his own Son. John took this connection even further, saying our love for others is a direct result of and proof of our love for God: "Whoever does not love does not know God, because God is love" (1 John 4:8). If we have been transformed by our surrender to God (Rom. 12:1–2), we will have a clear understanding of ourselves and our relationship to others (vv. 3–8), which will result in sincere, honest devotion to others (vv. 9–10). The deeper your love for God, the deeper will be your love for others. That kind of love will be a priority in our lives.

Even people who have surrendered to God at a deep level may struggle with loving others in this way, however. It is not that they lack sincerity or that they are unwilling to be honest in relationships. We face a barrier to intimacy in our culture that is pervasive, powerful, yet seemingly innocuous. That barrier is busyness. "I'd like to spend more time with so-and-so, but I'm just too busy." "I'd like to be part of a mentoring group, but who has the time?" Most of us have crowded calendars and relational waiting lists. There are people we would love to connect with, but they'll just have to stand in line until we're free. Perhaps the most dangerous aspect of this phenomenon is that we actually derive a sense of well-being from our frenetic activity, even as it chokes off relationships. After all, if we're busy, we must be doing something right. Only important people are in demand.

Richard Swenson, author of *Margin,* identifies four "gears" in which we live our lives: overdrive, drive, low, and park.[1] Most of us would probably admit we are in drive or overdrive most of the time, slowing into low gear only on some weekends and into park perhaps on holidays or vacations. However, it is nearly impossible to develop relationships while living at that pace, because we are driven to "make every moment count." We try to schedule "quality time" with friends, fellow church members, or family members, but those occasions often seem forced and produce little result. In relationships, the moments that count are often found among the moments that don't seem to count. Quality time nearly always emerges from spending a quantity of time together. To spend that time, which seems wasted by some standards, requires a decision to make relationships a priority.

Paul's term *honor* in verse 10 is based on a Greek word that literally means "to come after." To honor others here means to put them ahead of yourself. It means saying "you first" in the deepest sense, letting another go before or lead. This is not flattery, simply giving the most important seats or titles to others. It is placing others first in more important ways by meeting their needs before your own. Elsewhere Paul put it like this: "Do nothing out of selfish ambition or vain conceit. Rather, in humility value others above yourselves, not looking to your own interests but each of you to the interests of the others" (Phil. 2:3–4).

All of this requires intentionality. To deepen our relationships with others, we must carve out the time and energy to make room for others in our lives. That won't happen by accident, and the noxious weed of busyness will quickly reinvade our schedules if not continually pruned. Loving others means giving them priority not just in our schedules but also in our hearts, placing their needs ahead of our own. Deeper love requires an act of the will. This is something we choose to do for others.

What If?

Recalling my offering plate moment of 1999, the simmering conflict that led to it and the bruising fallout that followed, I can't help but imagine how differently things might have progressed had I been willing sooner to love others sincerely, honestly, and with priority. What if I had been less concerned with protecting my own insecurities? Would I have been more willing to engage in honest communication earlier, potentially snuffing out conflict before it could grow? If I had been more willing to cling to what is good and run from what is evil, would I have confronted divisive or manipulative behaviors immediately, caring more about the health of the body than about the reactions of a few individuals? Would I have placed a priority on the needs of others, including the congregation as a whole, so that I was willing to risk my own discomfort to put their needs first?

I will never know what might have been, yet I can say, based on my reflections over many years, that this offering plate moment led me to engage with others at a level of transparency and honesty I seldom had done before. That had a transforming effect on my personal life, my ministry, and my marriage and family. Surrender transforms relationships.

What if you were to surrender to God at a deeper level so your perfect love for him became deeper love for others? How would that affect your life, ministry, church, family, and community? There is only one way to find out.

_13_

Those Who Look Like Me vs. Those Who Are Different

OUR WONDERFULLY
DIVERSE COMMUNITY
WOULD BE REFLECTED
IN OUR CONGREGATION,
ALL FOR THE GLORY
OF GOD.

August 2005

I always look forward to the Global Leadership Summit simulcast. Held in August, this annual event presents a lineup of outstanding speakers. Kentwood Community Church (KCC) has been a host site for the simulcast that has originated from Willow Creek Community Church since 2000. I love the opportunity to connect informally with other church leaders. It's the perfect way to inspire our team for the ministry year ahead.

The 2005 event focused on the theme, "The Leader's State of Mind," and I was particularly attentive because I have a keen interest in intellectual development. As several hundred church leaders from the Grand Rapids region gathered in our worship center, I took a seat near the front alongside Kyle Ray. At the time, they were one of the few African American couples in our church. As lay leaders, they had participated in our largely unsuccessful attempts at becoming a more inclusive congregation. When Kyle sensed a call to ministry, he left his successful engineering career and enrolled at Asbury Theological Seminary in Kentucky. He and I kept in touch nearly every month while he was away. He was back in town to attend the simulcast and visit with friends.

"This is going to be good," I said as the simulcast began.

Kyle nodded agreement. "I'm really interested in this session on holy discontent."

I was too. Bill Hybels was the speaker, and he never failed to inspire. His powerful presentation identified the difference between holy and ordinary discontent. The holy variety is when something that concerns our heart also concerns the heart of God. Unlike ordinary discontent, which we seek to resolve quickly, the holy variety must be fed until it grows into an irresistibly compelling call to action. During the session, I made some notes about the possible intersections of my own discontent and the heart of God. Nothing really jumped out at me. Our church had come through the difficult time it had experienced five years earlier and was healthier than ever. We hit three thousand in weekend worship attendance, we had a great staff in place, and things were good. I didn't have much to be discontented with. "This is still a great session," I thought. "Maybe Kyle or some of the other leaders will benefit from it."

At the close of the session, Bill gave us some quiet time to ponder what our holy discontent might be. It was the typical commitment time that many speakers, especially pastors, include at the end of their message. I started mentally composing an agenda for our staff meeting. I was pretty much done with the topic of holy discontent.

But God wasn't. He broke through my condescending attitude with a simple question that poked a huge hole in my smug sense of contentment: "Wayne, does your church exist only for the people who look like you, or is it also a church for people who are different from you?"

I squirmed in my seat, thinking of Kyle, sitting next to me, and the valiant way he'd tried to make KCC a more comfortable place for African Americans, Hispanics, and the growing number of immigrants who called Kentwood home. When we began KCC in 1979, Kentwood was an emerging suburb on the southeast side of Grand Rapids. The city, incorporated just a dozen years before our church launched, was growing fast thanks to outstanding public schools and an expanding housing market. The population was 98 percent white, and 78 percent of those were of Dutch descent. Kentwood had a homogenous culture, which extended into church life. Congregations that were Dutch in culture and Reformed in theology were the norm.

Over the succeeding twenty-five years, however, new suburbs formed throughout Kent County. Kentwood became a first-ring suburb with new communities forming beyond it. The mostly white, mostly Dutch population began to move out of Kentwood and into those newer suburbs. The population of Kentwood became more diverse. Its public schools were now attended by children born in more than seventy countries and speaking dozens of native languages.

There had been a few times when God awakened me to that reality. I remember sitting in the grandstand for the commencement ceremony when my oldest son graduated from East Kentwood High School in 1999. As the students' names were called and they crossed the platform, I thought, "Wow, this is like sitting in the United Nations." Fully one-third of the class was comprised of students of color, and a significant portion of those students had been born outside the United States. Even so, I didn't catch the disconnect between the community, which was now about 30 percent minority, and our church, which remained about 98 percent white. We were no longer a monocultural community, but KCC was still a monocultural church.

"Well, we're doing our best," I told God. "We tried to become more diverse, but it didn't work. At least we're reaching more people than ever."

God was unimpressed. "Wayne, if you only care about the people who look, think, and act like you, at least have the integrity to stand before the congregation and say so. Tell them, 'KCC exists to reach white people. As for the rest of the community, let somebody else deal with them.'"

That seemed like a low blow, especially coming from the Lord, but I knew it was the truth. I was concerned. I won't say I was feeling holy discontent; maybe something more like panic. Either way, I was too uncomfortable to do nothing. Then I had a brainstorm. I saw a way to settle this whole thing right on the spot. I turned to Kyle.

"I've got an idea," I said. "When you graduate from seminary next spring, I'd like you to consider coming back to KCC as our outreach pastor. The Lord has recently impressed on me that we need to reach the full breadth of the residents in our community." I wasn't exactly culturally savvy, but even I knew better than to say "reach the black people" to an African American man.

I was sincere in making that offer to Kyle, but it was a classic surrender-avoidance move. Like Jonah, hopping into a boat bound for Tarshish, I was looking for an out, a way to do *something* without confronting my trepidation at leading my congregation in a direction I knew nothing about. I was a white guy who had grown up in an all white town, attended an all white college, and planted an all white church in an all white city. I was the definition of monocultural, and I had no idea how to lead a multicultural church.

I smiled encouragingly at Kyle, but he didn't exactly grin back. "Wayne, you know I respect you and love KCC," he began. I could feel a "but" coming. "But if you're looking for me to be the designated diversity guy, I'm not interested. You've been here since this church began. This transition can't happen unless the people know this comes from your heart and that you're willing to pay the price."

"Thanks a lot, pal," I thought to myself, but I kept smiling. I knew Kyle was right. Cultural diversity isn't something you can delegate. I also knew God would have to do a deep work in me before I would be ready to lead on this issue. I had attitudes, biases, and prejudices that were managed but not resolved. I knew others in the congregation did too. There would be opposition, and some people would choose to leave. I thought back to 1999 and the painful pruning the church had endured in those days. "I'm not ready to go through that again," I thought. "Not yet, Lord."

Surrender means transcending comfort zones, uprooting places where culture trumps Christ, releasing the familiar to embrace the unknown. That is never comfortable, and we often resort to avoidance mechanisms, sometimes quite sophisticated, as alternatives to surrender. In the days following the simulcast, the surrender battle escalated in my heart. In fact, God was working up a holy discontent within me. I just couldn't accept it. I could see that the community had changed and the church needed to change with it. But I had no idea how to lead that change. I knew how to lead a monocultural church; I'd been doing it for twenty-five years. But I was totally unprepared, spiritually and strategically, to lead a multiethnic church. I tried another avoidance maneuver.

The church was healthy and still growing, so I reasoned that we must be doing something right. Also, a new expressway had been constructed near the church with a convenient exit, so our reach was greater than ever. "If it ain't broke, don't fix it," I thought. "We are becoming a regional church. We may not reach every single person in Kentwood, but we're having a wider impact than ever before. It would be wrong to slow this down."

Sometimes God's voice is crystal clear to me, almost as if his message is delivered verbatim. At other times I simply have a sense of his direction. That was the case in this instance. The Spirit of God forcefully reminded me that I had been called to this community for a lifetime. Skipping over Kentwood itself to reach people who lived beyond it would be a revision of my call at best, more likely a rejection. It would have been far more comfortable to become a regional church, but I knew that was not my call. Another defensive tactic had been defeated. I could not ignore the diversity of Kentwood. I could not delegate the creation of a multicultural vision to staff members. I could not alter my mission to avoid dealing with the community to which God had specifically called me twenty-five years earlier. What could I do?

My defenses finally broken down, I laid all of my uncertainty before my heavenly Father. In prayer, I was led to Revelation 7:9. "After this I looked, and there before me was a great multitude that no one could count, from every nation, tribe, people and language, standing before the throne and before the Lamb." Finally, I was able to see the vision God has for his kingdom, and it is the same as the vision he had for KCC and for me. God wanted a bit of heaven to come right here on earth. He desired for his kingdom to come, his will to be done, in Kentwood as it is in heaven. He wanted us to go and make disciples of all nations, meaning all ethnicities or people groups. For us, the nations were now our neighbors. We must become a church for all of them.

At last I was able to surrender my uncertainty and insecurity and embrace God's vision.

I wanted to lead well and to be obedient to God's call. My preference is always to learn first, then lead, but I sensed urgency from the Holy Spirit on this matter. Though it had taken me years to see and follow God's direction, I would immediately begin leading others to embrace this new reality. Our wonderfully diverse community would be reflected in our congregation, all for the glory of God.

I knew the journey to becoming a multiethnic congregation would bring significant and potentially disruptive change, so I began slowly, sharing this vision with an inner circle of godly counselors to see if it resonated with them. When I found that it did, I next shared the vision with our board of elders, then our ministry staff. In January 2006, five months after my experience of holy discontent, our leaders adopted this goal: By 2020, KCC will be at least 20 percent diverse in weekend worship services.

Many aspects of this congregational journey go beyond the bounds of my own surrender and can be explored elsewhere. However, I will report this observation: when a matter of obedience requires not only my personal surrender but also the communal surrender of those I love and serve, I must be patient. God had been revealing this vision to me for years. I had been slow to see the need for change, so he repeated the revelation until I finally recognized and obeyed his voice. I didn't get it the first time, or the second time, or even the third time. I'm glad the Spirit persists in leading us into the process of surrender.

However, the surrender that had taken me years to make I now expected from the congregation in a matter of months. I shared a public message on the subject in February 2006, six months after my surrender experience. I spoke on the subject of loving our neighbors, and I used the message to relate my own journey and to unveil our goal to become a multiethnic congregation that reflected the reality of heaven here on earth. I promised we would journey together and travel at a speed that would allow everyone who wanted to join in to do so. I made it clear that our rate of climb would be adjustable but our destination would not. We would move steadily toward this God-honoring goal and would not be deterred.

Over the next several years, that resolve was tested as we said goodbye to people we loved who chose not to take part in the journey. At the same time, our joy was increased as we experienced a fellowship that exceeded sameness and was rooted in Christlikeness. I learned that the commission to "go and make disciples" is not only a mandate for evangelism, but also an opportunity for deeper discipleship. We can learn from those who are different from us, and I was profoundly changed by my relationship with people from whom I might be divided by culture. We were culturally different, but we were brought to unity through Christ. As of this writing, KCC's journey to diversity is more than a decade in progress, and the church has been profoundly changed as a result.

I know that the greatest change resulting from my surrender to God was not in the congregation or in the community, but in me. I discovered that going deeper with God not only deepened my relationships with others, it also broadened those relationships. As I became more fully surrendered to God, I became more open to the diversity of his gifts and calling among others. As my heart expanded, so did my vision for the world.

Surrender Widens Relationships

SHARE WITH THE LORD'S PEOPLE WHO ARE IN NEED. PRACTICE HOSPITALITY. BLESS THOSE WHO PERSECUTE YOU; BLESS AND DO NOT CURSE. REJOICE WITH THOSE WHO REJOICE; MOURN WITH THOSE WHO MOURN. LIVE IN HARMONY WITH ONE ANOTHER.

ROMANS 12:13

Through my offering plate moment in 1999, I discovered that surrender to God deepens relationships with others. I can no longer hide my true self, relate to others based on my need for self-protection, or fail to speak the truth because I fear the result. The deeper I go into the heart of God, the deeper will be my relationships with others. True love is deep love. We see this in the way God speaks about his love. "But God demonstrates his own love for us in this:

"While we were still sinners, Christ died for us" (Rom. 5:8). That's deep love.

God's love is also wide, meaning that it is expansive, inclusive. Scripture teaches us this as well. "For God so loved the world that he gave his one and only Son, that whoever believes in him shall not perish but have eternal life" (John 3:16). God's love includes everyone. It is as broad as it is deep, wide enough to include the whole world. And our love for others must be broad as well. That was the lesson from my moment of surrender in 2005. It was not enough for me to go deep in my relationships with the people who were closest to me—family members, staff members, friends, treasured church members. If my deeper love for God is to mirror his love for me, then it must widen to include others, many, many others, people who think and act and speak and dress and look and worship much differently than I do. The practice of that kind of love stretched me in ways I hadn't imagined. But I discovered that love is always a good thing, always beneficial and satisfying. Broad love, which includes those who are different from myself, is just as enriching as deep love, developing intimacy with those closest to me.

This should be no surprise because Paul traced this progression in his teaching on surrender in Romans 12. When we surrender to God (vv. 1–2), we become more aware of ourselves and others (vv. 3–8). This awareness leads to sincerity and honesty in relationships— a deeper love of others (vv. 9–12). And that brings us to the next aspect of surrender: we become *more* open to others. Our love widens to include everyone (vv. 13–20).

Anyone who has been drawn to this wider kind of love will tell you it is immensely challenging. Deeper love causes us to do away with the hypocrisy caused by insecurity or self-protection and be completely sincere with others, which is frightening in its own way. Broader love causes us to move out of our comfort zone to experience new situations, different ways of thinking, ideas that challenge us, and practices that threaten us, all while remaining rooted in our strong sense of identity (that is, "sober judgment" about ourselves). This, too, is intimidating. As if that weren't challenging enough, this wider love must include even relationships that have wounded us in the past, for unresolved conflicts have the potential to prevent our full surrender to God.

So how do we navigate the uncertain territory that lies beyond our comfort zone? What did Paul tell us that can equip us to engage with those who are different from us or even hostile to us? We must get beyond our need for familiarity and similarity, and beyond our desire to avoid difficulty. And all of that begins with getting beyond our primary obstacle to love ourselves.

Beyond Ourselves

Let's return for a moment to Romans 12:3–8, where Paul introduced the idea that our personal transformation produced transformation in our dealings with others. These verses show that our right thinking (*orthodoxy*) will be translated into right acting (*orthopraxy*). We will be appropriately humble about ourselves (v. 3) and will act out our God-given role (v. 4) for the benefit of all (vv. 6–8). A critical hinge in this passage lies in verse 5: "So in Christ we, though many, form one body, and each member belongs to all the others." To widen our relationships to include others, we must first get over the equally disastrous ideas that (a) we don't need others or that (b) others don't need us. In short, we have to get over ourselves. That brings us immediately to the concept of unity.

Unity

We are one body. That idea is mentioned twice in Romans 12 (vv. 4, 5) and is more fully stated in 1 Corinthians 12. Paul's metaphor powerfully makes the case for Christian unity. As the old spiritual goes—

> Knee bone connected to the thigh bone
> Thigh bone connected to the hip bone . . .
> ....
> Shoulder bone connected to the neck bone
> Neck bone connected to the head bone
> Now hear the word of the Lord.[1]

There can be no thought of separating oneself from the body and remaining alive. And if the metaphor itself doesn't make that clear, Paul states it explicitly: "The eye cannot say to the hand, 'I don't need you!' And the head cannot say to the feet, 'I don't need you!'" (1 Cor. 12:21). Each of us has a part in the body, and each one of us needs the entire body in order to function. There can be no such thing as a solitary Christian.

Our connection is for the benefit of other believers, but not for their benefit alone. It is true that the emphasis in Romans 12 is on the exercise of spiritual gifts, which is the common good. But John Wesley recognized as well the benefit of connection on the individual. He organized converts into societies (large groups) and a system of classes and bands (small groups) precisely because he understood that we need each other. On visiting one county in Wales, he wrote in his journal—

> I was more convinced than ever, that the preaching
> like an Apostle, without joining together those that are
> awakened, and training them up in the ways of God,
> is only begetting children for the murderer. How much
> preaching has there been for these twenty years all over

Pembrokeshire! But no regular societies, no discipline, no order or connection; and the consequence is, that nine in ten of the once-awakened are now faster asleep than ever.[2]

The pull of individualism is strong in our culture. It causes us to resist connections, especially deep ones. The power of ethnocentrism is equally strong. It causes us to resist broader connections with those who are different from us. If a Christian has something to learn from other Christians, it is also true that groups of Christians have something to learn from other groups of Christians. The white church is connected to the black church. The black church is connected to the Hispanic church. The North American church is connected to the African church. Now hear the word of the Lord!

Diversity

The body must be unified, but it must also be diverse. Each part is different and serves a different function. The body cannot be all hands or all eyes or all feet. Each part is needed. We have different gifts according to the grace given to each of us (Rom. 12:3–4). We each have a different passion, and that can be a source of frustration among us, as it was at Corinth. We wonder, "Why doesn't everyone feel the way I do?" or "Why am I not needed or valued in the way others are?" These differences should actually be a source of freedom. We are needed. Each one is important. And we are free to focus on what God has gifted us to do without trying to cover the bases assigned to others. Verses six through eight give us just a hint of the diversity of gifts within the body: prophesying, serving, teaching, leading, showing mercy, encouraging. No group could function well without the exercise of each of these gifts and many more. Within the body we are both valued for who we are and free to be exactly that.

To be open to wider relationships, we must admit we cannot do it all and don't have to. It can be challenging to see that truth as it relates to us personally. It can be even harder to draw that conclusion regarding our corporate selves. Yet I am convinced that this same principle applies to groups of Christians—denominations, congregations, parachurch organizations. Each of us seems to have a particular strength, just as each believer has a spiritual gift. The North American church seems to have been gifted with administration. We are terribly good at organizing things and fixing problems. Yet some of our sister churches seem far more gifted in things like prophesying and showing mercy. We each have a contribution to make to the others and to the global body of Christ. As individuals and as groups, we must get over the idea that we can be self-contained. The body needs diversity.

To make these broader connections within the body of Christ, we must get over ourselves and get beyond ourselves to make a sober judgment about our place in the widest possible context, the body of Christ. We must move beyond the shallow thinking that says, "I don't need others," and the self-pitying thought that "I'm not needed." This will allow us to embrace our role in the body, seeing ourselves in the context of others. This is the first step to widening our relationships.

Beyond Familiarity

Widening our relationships will immediately move us beyond the familiar, or as we would say it, beyond our comfort zone. Paul introduced this idea with the command to share with others and show hospitality (v. 13). The word for share here is *koinonia,* the biblical word for fellowship. The basic idea behind this term is having something in common. Sharing with those in need could mean two things, and probably means both. First, it could mean empathizing with the troubles of others, entering into their suffering with them. To do so takes us out of our safe, familiar environment into the painful, often chaotic, circumstances of others' lives. To even listen authentically to the suffering of others can be a difficult thing. To spend time with them, live alongside them, and enter into their circumstances with them will move you into unfamiliar places.

The second notion of sharing here is that of sharing resources, or generosity. Fellowship at its best includes empathy and action. This, too, will take us beyond what is familiar to us. Sharing our resources for the needs of others does not come naturally, especially when the needy people in question are different from us. We're likely to wonder, "Why don't they look after their own people?" or "How will I have enough for my family if I keep bailing out others?" Notice how the differences between us can become divisions when money is involved. Paul would not allow that kind of us-versus-them thinking in the church, however. He wrote to the Galatians, "So in Christ Jesus you are all children of God through faith, for all of you who were baptized into Christ have clothed yourselves with Christ. There is neither Jew nor Gentile, neither slave nor free, nor is there male and female, for you are all one in Christ Jesus. If you belong to Christ, then you are Abraham's seed, and heirs according to the promise" (3:26–29). Ethnicity, class, gender—those distinctions cannot be applied in the church. Our identify in Christ trumps all differences. It is the ultimate affinity factor. We are one body, one fellowship.

If sharing with others puts a hole in the fence around our comfort zone, the practice of hospitality rips it apart. Hospitality literally means pursuing the love of strangers, which is contrasted with the concept of brotherly love mentioned earlier (v. 10). Hospitality extends the reach of fellowship beyond the household of faith. We share with our brothers and sisters in Christ, and we share with strangers too. We think of hospitality as entertaining guests for a meal, and that harks back to the original concept. To show hospitality in the ancient world was to bring strangers in overnight. The basic idea here is to welcome the stranger. That could include assisting refugees, providing a meal for hungry people, or offering shelter to someone in need. In a broader sense, we show hospitality whenever we make others welcome in our presence. It is possible to practice hospitality at work, at church, at school, or in any context where there are outsiders.

Welcoming people you don't know into your personal space, whether at a lunch table, a worship center, or a living room, is challenging. But it is not optional. In addition to Romans 12, at least four other passages enjoin this responsibility. The writer of Hebrews says, "Do not forget to show hospitality to strangers, for by so doing some people have shown hospitality to angels without knowing it" (Heb. 13:2), and Peter writes, "Offer hospitality to one another without grumbling" (1 Pet. 4:9). Paul twice listed being hospitable as a requirement for church leadership (1 Tim. 3:2, Titus 1:8).

A common misconception holds that the larger congregations that have become more common in recent years are places where one can avoid deeper, wider relationships. Some people believe a large church is a place where they can hide in a crowd, thereby avoiding relationships, or where their presence would go unnoticed, causing them to miss out on relational intimacy. That has not been the case in my experience, and most church leaders I know are diligent about gathering attendees into contexts in which they will both be known and loved and will be responsible to know and love others. The fact that we live in a generally more affluent culture and have the means to keep others at a distance through technology does not absolve us from the biblical injunction to love.

Churches nearly always have some list of competencies and responsibilities for leaders. How would it change a church and its relationship to its community if it were a requirement that every pastoral staff member, board member, and ministry leader were held accountable to "pursue the love of strangers?" Our surrender to God must lead us into wider relationships with others. To do so, we will have to tolerate, even embrace, the discomfort of moving beyond the familiar.

Beyond Similarity

To widen our relationships, we must move beyond similarity. This key concept is highlighted by Paul's use of the word *harmony* (Rom. 12:16). If we are to live in harmony, we must accept the idea that differences are not only tolerable but also desirable. When each member of the choir sings the identical note, you have unison. Harmony occurs when members sing different notes that follow the same theme. Harmony cannot happen without variety.

To live in harmony will mean identifying with people in a *variety of situations.* We rejoice with those who rejoice and mourn with those who mourn (v. 15). Typically, we are most comfortable associating ourselves with those whose emotional range or current experience most closely matches our own. Misery loves company, as the saying goes. So when we are sad, we want everyone crying along in unison. When we're angry, we want others to share our outrage. Optimists tend to flock together, and so do complainers. Living in harmony means stretching outside the sameness of your own temperament or current experience to enter into the lives of those who are different. We don't only celebrate or only mourn, but we enter into either experience with others when appropriate. For some, this means developing an emotional range that is unfamiliar. Rather than withdraw from others, we engage with them.

Moving beyond similarity also means associating with people in a *variety of positions.* Paul wrote, "Do not be proud, but be willing to associate with people of low position" (v. 16). He might also have added the reverse instruction as well. Those in low positions must not think themselves somehow superior to those who are above them. The phrase translated "live in harmony with one another" literally means to think the same thing toward one another (v. 16). The apostle James drove home a finer point on this, saying, "Believers in our glorious Lord Jesus Christ must not show favoritism" (James 2:1).

Some people have trouble relating up, that is, to people whom they perceive to be above them in position, status, education, or economic standing. Others have a harder time relating down to those whom they think of as lower in status. Broadening our relationships means either lifting or lowering our eyes to see and care about those who seem to have a different standing than our own. If rejoicing and mourning (v. 15) represent the emotional highs and lows of relationships, social status presents us with positional highs and lows. Jesus exercised the power of recognition, sharing a table with those of high standing, like Simon the Pharisee (Luke 7:36–50), and low standing, like Levi the tax collector (5:27–32). We must be willing to do the same.

Paul's admonition "Do not be proud" (Rom. 12:16) echoes the earlier advice, "Do not think of yourself more highly than you ought, but rather think of yourself with sober judgment, in accordance with the faith God has distributed to each of you" (v. 3). Our position in life is not our own doing. When we recognize the blessings of God and the realities of privilege that our status bestows, we are more willing to widen our associations with others. Personally, it took some time to become aware of the advantages I have enjoyed in life because of my race, gender, positive home life, and nationality. Realizing these accidents of birth provide advantages I have not earned, I am much more humble about my situation in life and much more open to those who have not had similar privileges.

Beyond Difficulty

Moving beyond familiarity and similarity can be challenging. We tend to become uncomfortable in new situations, and relating to those who are different from ourselves places us in such situations. According to Paul, when we surrender ourselves fully to God and mirror his love for the world, we must move beyond the problems we have had in dealing with others. Unresolved relational conflicts are a barrier to full surrender. To widen our love for others, we must move beyond difficulty.

Broken relationships create wounds and cause us to withdraw into ourselves. This defensiveness can undo the progress we have made by getting beyond ourselves, beyond familiarity and similarity. Paul pulled no punches here. He made it clear that our love for God must extend not only to those who are different from us but also to those who have wounded us. "Do not repay anyone evil for evil. Be careful to do what is right in the eyes of everyone. If it is possible, as far as it depends on you, live at peace with everyone. Do not take revenge" (vv. 17–19).

I want to pause here and say clearly that this is not a call to tolerate abusive behavior. Instead, this is an imperative to refuse answering harm with harm and to live peaceably with others. There are cases where that is not possible because the other party refuses to repent or even acknowledge the injury. Paul was exhorting us to make an honest effort to forgive grievances and live in peace. This does not mean remaining silent when others continue to do wrong or allow ourselves to be victimized.

You may already know which relationships have been disruptive in your life. What you may not realize is the depth of the damage this has done to your soul. Unresolved conflicts in relationships with others nearly always affect our relationship with God. This checklist may help you identify the areas of woundedness in your heart.

- *Do I find myself unable to bless others?* "Bless those who persecute you; bless and do not curse" (v. 14).
- *Am I preoccupied with revenge?* "Do not repay anyone evil for evil. . . . Do not take revenge, my dear friends, but leave room for God's wrath, for it is written: 'It is mine to avenge; I will repay,' says the Lord" (vv. 17, 19).
- *Do I treat people differently depending on who is looking?* "Be careful to do what is right in the eyes of everyone" (v. 17).
- *Am I unwilling to do my part in resolving the conflict?* "If it is possible, as far as it depends on you, live at peace with everyone" (v. 18).
- *Am I unwilling to meet another's legitimate needs?* "If your enemy is hungry, feed him; if he is thirsty, give him something to drink. In doing this, you will heap burning coals on his head" (v. 20).
- *Am I becoming consumed with evil rather than good?* "Do not be overcome by evil, but overcome evil with good" (v. 21).

If your answer to even one of these questions is yes, a broken relationship is damaging your own relationship with God.

Paul also gave us signs of willingness to be reconciled in relationships.

- *Am I focused on pursuing righteousness over seeking revenge* (v. 21)?
- *Am I willing to do my part to create a peaceful relationship* (v. 18)?

The phrase "as far as it depends on you" is critical to applying this command. The actions and reactions of others are always beyond our control. Trying to control those things often contributes to the breach of relationships. We may try to control others passively, by refusing to share our feelings or by ignoring others, or we may attempt active control by being demanding or confrontational. Paul was wise enough to acknowledge that some relationships cannot be repaired. Yet we always have the power to end conflict on our side by being honest, apologizing or asking for apology, refusing to seek retribution, or disengaging from contentious people or situations. The key is willingness to do what does lie within our power, though that may sometimes be difficult.

The failure to address conflict can be just as damaging as furthering conflict. Edwin Friedman coined the phrase *peacemonger* to describe the destruction caused by some well-intentioned leaders who lack the nerve to actively mend broken relationships. Our culture favors false harmony and good feelings over progress and integrity. This peace-at-all-costs mentality actually produces a false peace in which broken relationships continue to fester. Our challenge is to be peacemakers without becoming peacemongers. To do so, we must make critical decisions.

First, we must actively place our trust in God to bring justice. If we believe the promise, "'It is mine to avenge; I will repay,' says the Lord" (v. 19), we are able to pursue reconciliation without demanding vengeance. This requires a surrender of our right to revenge, trusting instead that God will do what is necessary to bring justice. This does not necessarily mean a victim should pursue relational depth with a victimizer. We can end a conflict and still leave room for God's vengeance. This is a tremendously difficult offering plate moment for those who have been grievously wronged.

Second, we must choose to overcome evil with good (v. 21). This is possible based on the belief that God's justice will in fact prevail. Love is a stronger power than hate. Truth is stronger than falsehood. Forgiveness trumps vengeance. To overcome evil with good is an active choice. It requires choosing obedience over our personal style of conflict resolution. Most people deal with conflict in one of five ways. They either compete, withdraw, surrender, compromise, or resolve. Overcoming evil with good may require an action that takes us beyond our emotional comfort zone.

Open Arms

Reflecting on my offering plate moment in 2005, I realize I had been operating from a limited relational range. As someone who had lived my entire life in monocultural settings, I had a low desire to engage with those who were either unfamiliar or dissimilar to me. It isn't that I bore them ill will. My surrender to God simply wasn't yet deep enough to fully mirror his love for others—a love that is as wide as it is deep. I needed to get beyond myself in order to open my heart to those who were different from me ethnically, generationally, economically, and in other ways. As I began to do that, I made some rookie mistakes. Not every contact with strangers—those who are different from and unknown to me—blossomed into friendship. I unwittingly gave offense at times. I learned, and I grew. And I developed not a mere a tolerance for going beyond my relational range but a delight in doing so. Loving others enriches our lives. It never diminishes them.

Each of us seems to have a relational range, a spectrum of people with whom we feel comfortable. It takes the average person only a second or two to assess a newcomer according to that relational comfort zone. With barely a glance we determine whether or not we will be open to a relationship with that person. Widening our love for others requires widening that range. It requires us to suspend judgment based on external factors such as race, economic standing, national origin, gender, language, modes of dress, and marital history. We must intentionally connect with those we have yet to know. We must seek relationships that broaden our relational range. When we do so, we find many people from whom we had been segregated by these arbitrary factors will be welcomed into our fellowship and into our hearts. Our arms are wider than we think.

What You Do vs. Who God Is

BETWEEN THE
COMMAND TO
"GO" AND THE
ASSURANCE
"I WILL SHOW"
LIES A HUGE
"I DON'T KNOW."

July 2009

July is normally a slow time in church life. Parishioners travel. Staff members squeeze in a vacation before the start of fall ministries. Attendance dips temporarily. July would normally have been a month when I take some time away to spend with family and seek God's direction for the next season of preaching. But our church board was meeting this month to discuss an urgent matter, one that I'd initiated, one that concerned my future and the future of Kentwood Community Church (KCC). It was about 8:30 on a Tuesday morning when Charles Montgomery, the lay leader of our congregation, stepped into my office and said, "Wayne, do you have a minute?" I was expecting his visit.

"The board met last night," he began, which of course I already knew. "And we made a decision." Here it came. "In the event of a vacancy in the office of senior pastor, we will recommend that Kyle Ray be elected as your successor."

I'd been bracing myself for this moment for months, but nothing could have prepared me for those words. I couldn't stop the tears from coming. At length I composed myself enough to respond. "Thank you for telling me," I said, walking him to the door. "I now know what I have to do."

The moment he left the room, I sat down at my desk and wrote a letter of resignation. After thirty years, my ministry at KCC had come to an end.

Looking back on the pivotal moments of surrender in my life, it appears that most of them have begun with food. There was the breakfast at Mr. Burger where Kevin Myers asked for my blessing in leaving KCC to plant a church in Atlanta. And the lunch at Arnie's where Jerry DeRuiter told me that the church board would challenge me to lead in a critical area I'd been avoiding. And there was that cookout with friends when I finally embraced Jan's leading on the question of adopting a child. I'm not sure that surrender *has* to include eating, but it certainly does involve the whole person. Maybe the way to the heart really is through the stomach. So it is no surprise that my most emotional moment of surrender, and one that most dramatically reshaped the course of my ministry, also began with food. It started on January 20, 2009, when I met Kyle Ray at a Kava House near KCC.

January 20 has been a significant day in my life since 1993, when our daughter, Elise, arrived from South Korea. We celebrate that each year as Gotcha Day, the day we embraced her into our lives. On January 20, 2003, our future daughter-in-law, Leila, committed her life to Jesus Christ. That became her spiritual Gotcha Day, the day she was adopted into God's family. I was thinking of these joyous beginnings as I walked into Kava House, one of the coolest little coffee shops in a neighborhood with more java joints than Christian bookstores, a real achievement in Grand Rapids.

Kyle and Petra had begun attending KCC when they moved to the community in 1999. After years of faithful service as lay leaders, Kyle sensed a call to ministry and went away to seminary for a few years. He had returned in 2006 as our outreach pastor, building bridges to individuals who had yet to know Christ and to our community as a whole. As an African American man who had spent most of his career in ethnically diverse settings, Kyle was a particular asset in helping our congregation become more inclusive. I considered him critical to reaching our goal of becoming 20 percent diverse in worship attendance by the year 2020. After talking through a number of ministry issues, Kyle changed the subject to a more personal matter.

"Wayne, I think this is my year," he said.

As had been the case with Kevin Myers in 1987, I'd been expecting a conversation like this with Kyle, though perhaps not quite so soon.

"You know that I've felt called to be a senior pastor at some point," Kyle went on. "During our Christmas Eve service, God let me know that 2009 would be my year to prepare for that role."

Kyle was an exceptionally effective staff member, and his gift for preaching was increasingly evident. I had hoped he would stay with us bit longer, but our congregation was committed to helping emerging leaders find their best place of kingdom contribution. I was happy to talk about his future plans. At the moment, Kyle was simply asking for coaching in areas unique to the role of senior pastor, such as leading a board, directing staff, and creating and casting vision. I was more than willing to provide that coaching, but in that conversation I felt prompted to challenge Kyle with a question. I asked him, "Do you feel called to this church and this community?"

"I never really thought about that," he said. "I know I'm called to be a senior pastor, and I know that you're called to this church for a lifetime. So I guess staying here never really crossed my mind."

I had been very open with our leadership team about my lifetime call to Kentwood and to KCC. In fact, I'd recently led the board in creating a strategic plan for the upcoming decade. I had no thought of leaving. Kyle and I agreed to revisit the question of his call in a future conversation, and I encouraged him to give it some thought. Did he feel specifically called to the city of Kentwood and to KCC? We finished our coffee and headed back to the office.

I all but forgot about that conversation until a couple months later, when Kyle and I were back at Kava House and once again discussing the role of a senior pastor. Recalling our previous talk, I asked, "So did you and Petra pray about whether or not you feel called to this community and this church?"

"We did," Kyle said. "And we do. But I don't know what to do with that. I know I am to be a senior pastor, and I do feel called to KCC." He paused, hesitating to say what we both were thinking. "But you're the pastor here."

"I don't know what to make of it either," I said, and I truly didn't. But I did have a sense that God was up to something. Now it was my turn to ask my spouse to pray with me about God's leading for the future. Over the next few weeks, Jan and I prayed about our place at KCC. Every time I prayed, I found myself weeping. I normally process things intellectually rather than emotionally, so I was puzzled about this. "Why am I such an emotional wreck?" I kept asking myself. It didn't make sense.

Slowly, I began to piece together what was happening in my mind and heart. I've often told people that it wasn't only our children who grew up at KCC. Jan and I did too. We'd just been kids when I became pastor, fresh out of college. The thirty years that followed included every significant event in our lives. We'd grown together as a couple, become parents, adopted a child. We'd shared the highs and lows of planting a church, the difficult struggles and the great triumphs. This church had been our life. And it was my entire career, the only full-time ministry job I'd ever had. Finally, it hit me. I was being released. "My time at KCC is coming to a close," I realized. "I'm about to leave the only ministry I've ever known." No wonder I was emotionally volatile. I was grieving the loss of one of the most important relationships in my life, a pastor's relationship with a congregation.

Ten years prior to my feeling of being released from KCC, I had worked with the church board to develop a succession plan.

I did that because I'd seen what happens when beloved pastors stay too long, undermining the good work they've accomplished by outstaying God's call. I'd always prayed that when my time at KCC was done, God would make it clear to me. I loved my work there, but I knew it would someday come to an end. I wanted to welcome that day when it arrived, rather than deny or avoid it. However, some experiences are much easier to write into a strategic plan than they are to live. When I realized the day of my departure was upon me, the emotions and insecurities I'd tried to plan out of existence swept over me with incredible force. It was impossible to rely on the surrender I'd made ten years ago when I created a transition plan. I needed fresh submission to God's will.

Ten years earlier, while creating the succession plan, I had observed the various ways pastors reacted when they sensed a transition coming. I'd noticed that some pastors would begin by seeking out or being offered other ministry opportunities. Their sense of release followed their call to the next thing. Other pastors first experienced a sense of release and only later dis-covered God's next step for their ministry. I had concluded that I was more of a "release first" person, so I had never seriously considered other ministry possibilities. For thirty years I had thought about nothing other than pastoring KCC. So when I accepted the idea that I had been released from KCC, the divine sense of completion led immediately to a dreadful sense of uncertainty. I had no clue as to what came next.

Over the next few months, I began to think of this experience as my own Abrahamic adventure. Abraham left his home to go to a place the Lord would reveal to him only later. I was doing something similar. What I discovered is that between the command to "Go" and the assurance "I will show" lies a huge "I don't know." The uncertainty I experienced during those weeks inflamed my predisposition to insecurity. The need to surrender now engulfed all aspects of my life: spiritual, emotional, and practical. I would have to leave all of this in God's hands in order to initiate my transition away from KCC. The totality of that call to surrender called into question my very identity as a pastor and as a person.

Prior to this season, I would have said that my identity and my security were rooted in Christ, but this season of not knowing the future caused me to see that this was only partly true. For three decades I had been the lead pastor of a congregation that was highly visible and sometimes controversial in its community and its denomination. Sometimes people talked about us, wondering why we made the decisions we made. At other times they talked to us, asking how we'd been so successful in making disciples. In either case, KCC and I were the focal point of many conversations. Over time, my identity had become enmeshed with my role to a far greater degree than I'd realized. If I weren't the senior pastor of KCC, who was I? I wasn't sure I knew.

Years earlier, I'd heard leadership coach Dick Zalack say this: "The difference between leaders and followers is their capacity to live with uncertainty." That statement had made an impression on me, but in this season of uncertainty, I came to understand it differently. I learned that when Jesus invites me to come with him, uncertainty about circumstances is inescapable. I can't follow him and cling to my need for control. My sense of certainty can come only from the person and call of Christ, not my current circumstances or even my place in ministry.

I'd also heard Bill Hybels say that "we need to develop the capacity to sit in the uncertainty." Maybe that's what Mary the mother of Jesus was doing as she pondered in her heart the angelic birth announcement. Uncertainty is a difficult piece of real estate to occupy. We move on from it as quickly as we can. I'm usually tempted to trade the uncertainty that comes with living for what is ultimately certain for the mirage of certainty that comes from trying to control my own circumstances. During the time following my release from KCC, that temptation to grasp for control became almost overwhelming. As the weeks went by, the progression of my surrender moved from tears to what Paul described as "wordless groans." This was the most intense experience I'd ever had of needing to pray but not knowing how to pray. For the first time in my life, I came to depend on the Spirit of God to speak on my behalf (Rom. 8:26–27). This season of uncertainty called for a surrender that chipped away the superficial security that came from my dependence on a position or role to provide my sense of identity. I came to depend on Christ alone.

By June 2009, five months had passed since that first coffee-house conversation with Kyle. During that time my sense of release did not weaken but only strengthened. When our board met for its quarterly meeting in June, the Spirit prompted me to take a step that would push my surrender beyond the point of no return. I told the board that I had been released from KCC and would soon initiate a change. Our discussion was laced with emotion and required more than a few pauses for me to regain composure. I shared the story of my conversations with Kyle, the intense times of prayer, and my sense of release. I let them know I believed God was preparing the way for Kyle to lead our church. Some were confused, as I initially had been, because I had repeatedly told them I felt a lifetime call to KCC and had just led a strategic planning initiative. They wondered if I was

making a mistake. The depth of my emotion may have led some to wonder if I was facing some sort of personal crisis. I assured them that neither was the case. God had brought me to a deeper place of surrender, and I was following his unmistakable call on my life. The meeting was an emotional one, to say the least, but concluded with expressions of acceptance by the board.

That meeting resolved nothing, however. It merely marked what Winston Churchill might call "the end of the beginning." Both the board and I still had to find an answer to the question "What next?"

In The Wesleyan Church, a pastor does not arrange for his or her own succession. That authority rests with the church board, the district superintendent, and ultimately the congregation. While board members were moved by my story and trusted my sense of God's leading, they were bound to follow their own process in planning for the future. As one member put it, "We trust you, and we love Kyle. But we have to take seriously our responsibility to interview him and seek God's will about whether he should be our next pastor." So they began working with the district superintendent to outline an interview process.

Several weeks later, Charles Montgomery came to me with the board's decision. In the event of a vacancy in the role of senior pastor, Kyle would receive the board's unanimous nomination to fill the role. I offered my resignation that same day, with gratitude for the privilege of serving KCC for more than three decades.

In making that resignation, I had surrendered to God at the deepest and most gut-wrenching level yet, letting go of my treasured role as pastor of the church I'd planted and led for thirty years. But I still had no idea what would be next. I had already turned down a teaching position, feeling certain that the classroom was not the place for me. "Are you sure?" Jan asked. I knew she was weighing the possibility of moving away from the community and leaving a teaching position she loved and felt called to.

"Can you see me grading papers every evening?" I asked.

Meanwhile, Kyle and I shared our story with the KCC family in early August, and the board presented Kyle as its nominee for senior pastor. A few weeks, later, an overwhelming majority of the congregation elected Kyle,. The election was a clear indication of the church's love and respect for his leadership. Yet many were still concerned for Jan and me. Some felt anxiety on our behalf because we didn't yet know what our next step would be. One or two folk floated conspiracy theories, suggesting I'd been forced out. We managed to allay those concerns. Still, we wondered what would happen on the day after I concluded my service to KCC, which was coming closer day by day. As for me, my surrender had produced a sense of peace. I was concerned but not anxious about the future, believing we had clearly sensed God's will and made the right choice.

Then one day I got a call from Dr. Henry Smith, who was the president of Indiana Wesleyan University. "Wayne, I'm sure you're aware that we're launching a seminary here at Indiana Wesleyan," he said. "I'd like you to consider leading that effort."

I was flattered but disinterested. "I'm a pastor," I said. "That's all I've ever done. I have absolutely no experience in the administration of higher education."

"Exactly," he replied. "Wesley Seminary will be geared toward the practice of ministry, and we want a leader who has given his life to ministry in the local church and beyond."

Now he had my attention. I interviewed in early September, and, on the first weekend of October, during the celebration of KCC's thirtieth anniversary, Dr. Smith was present to announce my new role to the congregation: vice president of Wesley Seminary at Indiana Wesleyan University. I was blessed by the congregation's enthusiastic affirmation of the opportunity God was giving me to invest myself in equipping leaders for the kingdom.

This offering plate moment had been a refiner's fire, purifying the source of my security and identity. That refinement continued over the coming months as we said good-bye to the church I loved, then took on the challenge of learning to function in a completely different role. It felt like starting over. Seasons of surrender often do. For we can never step into the new thing God has for us until we are willing to surrender the old. Every beginning requires an end. In this case, it was the end of basing my self-image on a role or position. I had learned to depend on Christ alone.

Surrender Establishes the Fullness of the Spirit

Surrender begins and ends with the spirit. Our culture reinforces our natural tendency to make surrender purely a matter of the flesh, or body. Our temptation is to allow surrender to float on the surface, submitting certain behaviors to God's will but ignoring the soulish areas of mind, emotions, and volition, along with the deeper level of the spirit, the seat of our ultimate affections. Worldly surrender is mere behavior modification, bringing some aspect of our outer life into line with God's will while allowing the heart to remain in rebellion.

True surrender originates from a heart fully devoted to God. This establishes the Spirit-to-spirit connection that Paul described in Romans 8:16: "The Spirit himself testifies with our spirit that we are God's children." Such people are "led by the Spirit of God" (Rom. 8:14), not living in fear (v. 15) but enjoying the full confidence of favored children (v. 17). This deep connection with God enables us to know and do God's will in all aspects of life. This is what Paul meant when he wrote, "Then you will be able to test and approve what God's will is—his good, pleasing and perfect will" (12:2). Surrender makes that possible because surrender establishes a deep connection with the Father.

This is the surrender I struggled to make during my final days at Kentwood Community Church (KCC). This is not to say I had not previously surrendered to God or was living a dual life. Not at all! It is just that deep surrender takes time. The self finds many hiding places in the soul, even wrapping itself around good things like a call to ministry or service to a local church. When we are able to make this deeper surrender, we recognize self and selfishness more readily, and we follow God more confidently.

Elsewhere, Paul described this deeper surrender as a death experience that produces this same Spirit-to-spirit connection. "Those who belong to Christ Jesus have crucified the flesh with its passions and desires. Since we live by the Spirit, let us keep in step with the Spirit" (Gal. 5:24–25). As my offering plate moments experienced over many years well illustrate, this surrender is not a once-for-life event. We must continually crucify the self, surrendering our spirit to the Lord at deeper and deeper levels. As we do, we are increasingly connected with God and are able to "keep in step with the Spirit," meaning we are able to see God's will for our lives and consistently choose to do it.

What are the evidences of this Spirit-to-spirit connection in our lives? Or, what is the goal of our complete surrender to God? There are two. First, we know we have a Spirit-to-spirit connection when we are led by God. Second, we know we have this connection when we are loved by him.

We Are Led by God

The first evidence of surrender is that we are increasingly able to discern and do the will of God. We are led by the Spirit. This outworking of surrender sounds more complicated than it is. As our minds are transformed, our consciences are quickened and we find ourselves better able to recognize the Spirit's leading and are more willing to follow it. We begin to think more like God thinks.

Conviction

One of the first ways we experience this leading is through *conviction*. Conviction is having a sense of when God says no to something. God's revealed Word says no to a great number of things, including idolatry, sexual immorality, and murder. Beyond those clear prohibitions, however, we are left to exercise personal discernment on a great number of matters. We must learn to follow the Spirit's prompting. Even the apostles faced this in deciding, for example, whether to require Gentile converts to be circumcised, which was a requirement of the Mosaic law (see Acts 15) and whether eating meat that had been used in pagan sacrifices constituted idolatry (see 1 Cor. 8). Paul summarized the early church's handling of such matters in Romans 14:5: "Each of them should be fully convinced in their own mind." When there is no clear revelation on an issue, each person must follow his or her own convictions.

As we surrender more fully to God, it becomes easier to see when he is saying no on a particular issue. More to the point, it becomes easier and easier to follow that conviction. Often we understand the conviction God has given but resist acting upon it. Surrender enables us to personally say no to the things to which God has said no.

Convictions may be individual or they may be collective. On the matter of requiring Gentile converts to be circumcised, the early church established a collective conscience. Their decision was that circumcision should not be required for new converts but that all believers should "abstain from food polluted by idols, from sexual immorality, from the meat of strangled animals and from blood" (Acts 15:20). Individuals may have had a different personal conviction, but they agreed to abide by the collective conviction of the church. That requires yet a deeper level of surrender, to surrender one's own conscience to the leading of the body.

Affirmation

The flip side of conviction is *affirmation*, which is the ability to discern when God is saying yes. Surprisingly, this can be more difficult for some Christians to practice. Some have been so accustomed to thinking of God as angry, vindictive, and restrictive that they have a hard time imagining he could be in favor of anything. It takes a true Spirit-to-spirit connection for them to hear the yes in God's voice—yes to opportunities, yes to risks, yes to enjoyable experiences. It sometimes seems more pious to have a conviction than to feel an affirmation. We think of those who not only accept but also seek opportunities to deny themselves as being more holy. A deep act of surrender is required to help such folk become attuned to God's affirming voice.

Staying in Tune with the Spirit

Surrender enables us to hear the promptings of the Spirit, whether they are convicting or affirming. Any preacher can tell you of occasions when, following a sermon, a parishioner has said, "Pastor, when you said this, God really spoke to me." Yet the preacher had said no such thing. At other times, parishioners may say, "I feel like you wrote that message specifically for me. It's as if you had been listening to our dinnertime conversations this week." We preachers know such moments have nothing to do with us. Only God's Spirit can apply truth that specifically.

At times, staying in step with the Spirit means staying in touch with others. That's the case with collective conscience. And God's affirming voice may require hearing the promptings of God through others as well, as I discovered when Jan and I were considering adoption and when I was being released from my call to KCC. Listening for God's voice together builds intimacy among people because it requires openness to one another. In the case of Jan and me, we found there is great power in following God's voice together, even though we have different approaches to discerning that leading. I tend to focus on the big picture and then choose actions in accordance with it. Jan tends to look for the next right step to take, believing that God will lead us to the larger outcome through small, faithful actions. When we are able to sense God's leading together, the sense of conviction or affirmation is much stronger.

Responses to God's Leading

Our initial responses to hearing God speak directly to us may vary from person to person. Like some people mentioned in Scripture who heard God's voice directly, we may not respond positively at first. As we surrender more fully, we are able to respond more quickly. Here are three possible responses to the voice of God.

Cynicism. The young boy Samuel was unsure of what he was hearing when God first spoke to him (see 1 Sam. 3). Though he may not have been fully cynical, he was at least confused. He didn't know what to make of the experience. Others are downright skeptical of the idea that God may speak directly to human beings. We may think those who make such claims are manipulative at best, mentally disturbed at worst. In time, we may come to view the phrase, "God told me," with a bit of cynicism. That cynicism will shut down our ability to hear the voice of God.

Curiosity. Moses's response to God's voice is best described as curiosity (see Ex. 3). When he saw the burning bush, he decided to investigate. As God spoke, Moses formed a list of questions. He didn't question that God was speaking, but he certainly had questions about what would come next. Curiosity is not wrong, but it is possible to become so mired in questions about God or for God that we fail to obey God.

Certainty. Mary the mother of Jesus demonstrated a different response to the voice of God. She was immediately convinced (see Luke 1). Think also of David, on hearing a prophetic word of conviction through Nathan. David's repentance was immediate. This is the level of response we hope to arrive at through our surrender to God: full and immediate obedience to his voice. We recognize when the Spirit is speaking to us, and we respond without hesitation.

You may recall the film *Two Weeks Notice,* a story about a self-centered real estate developer who hires a savvy environmental lawyer who soon becomes his indispensable aide. However, she quits because she realizes how selfish and shallow he is. But the developer wins her back with a climactic speech that includes these words: "And even though I've said cruel things and driven her away, she's become the voice in my head. And I can't seem to drown her out. And I don't want to drown her out."[1] When we are fully surrendered to God, the

Spirit becomes the voice inside our head we cannot drown out and no longer want to. Though we may initially have been cynical or merely curious, we find ourselves fully convinced by the conviction or affirmation of his voice. We walk in step with the Spirit.

Spiritual Deafness

John the apostle walked with Jesus and learned from him when John was perhaps in his twenties. Decades later, exiled on the island of Patmos, John received a revelation from the Lord that was intended for the seven churches of Asia. To each one, he offered the revelation with this admonition: "Whoever has ears, let them hear what the Spirit says to the churches" (Rev. 2:7, 11, 17, 29; 3:6, 13, 22). John had learned to hear the voice of the Lord, even in a whisper, but he was writing to Christians who had become spiritually deaf. This shows us it is possible to miss hearing the voice of God despite having a relationship with him. John's message was given to rouse those whose spiritual sensitivity had become dulled by time and inattention. Jesus said, "Here I am! I stand at the door and knock. If anyone hears my voice and opens the door, I will come in and eat with that person, and they with me" (3:20).

Christ at the Door	
closed	open
deaf	alert
out of touch	in tune
what?	wow!

Though these words of Christ are often applied to evangelism, they were intended for Christians. It is imperative to keep
our ears attuned to the voice of God. Christ's knock is meant to
move us from spiritual deafness to attentiveness to the voice
of the Spirit.

Remember that the voice of the Spirit is not always affirming; sometimes it's convicting. Jesus said, "Those whom I love
I rebuke and discipline" (v. 19). Imagine Christ standing at the
door of your heart now. How might he complete this statement
if addressed to you? "Those whom I love I _____.
Many things may come to your mind: bless, affirm, protect,
enable. It is possible, perhaps likely, he would complete it in
some unexpected way. The words *rebuke* and *discipline* are
not heartwarming, but the Laodicean church needed them.
Remember that God disciplines those whom he loves (Heb.
12:6). If you've gone through a tough time lately, you may be
thinking, "Maybe God loves me a little too much!" He loves you
enough to get your attention.

Our best response to Christ's knocking on our heart's door
is to answer with earnest repentance. Jesus said, "Those
whom I love I rebuke and discipline. So be earnest and repent"
(Rev. 3:19). We "hear" and "open" to the Lord (see v. 20) by
becoming receptive to his call. As Paul reminds us, we do have
the ability to hear God's voice. That receptor was implanted in us
at salvation (see Rom. 8:16). We can either tune in or tune out.

Staying Receptive

The fact that Christ had to remind the Asian churches to
be open to his voice should inform us that this heart-tuning
requires frequent adjustment. Before the days of satellite
communication, listening to the radio on a long automobile trip
required periodic retuning of the car radio. As the signal from
one station faded in the distance, a driver had to scan the dial to
find another station that would come in stronger. Continued

listening required constant adjustment. We're on a lifelong spiritual journey, and frequent adjustment of the heart may be needed to keep the signal strong. That requires spiritual training. We must train ourselves to hear the voice of God.

Some musicians have a marvelous ability known as *perfect pitch.* Many of us who are not musically inclined cannot tell one note from another, even with printed music in front of us. Some gifted individuals are able to distinguish one note from all others with no outside aid. On hearing a police siren, they can tell you if it sounds the note A or E. When hearing a piano, they can hear even one string that is slightly out of tune. Spiritually, it is possible to train your heart to have perfect pitch. With practice, prayer, and discernment, it is possible to distinguish the voice of the Spirit among all others.

One way to do that is through the practice of personal spiritual disciplines. The most frequently practiced are those we program into our quiet time or personal devotions. Through Scripture reading, prayer (including listening, not just speaking), journaling, and theological reflection, we become more attuned to the Spirit's voice.

Other people can be a great aid in our development of spiritual listening. Spiritual relationships such as accountability partners, mentors, or spiritual directors can be a "clearness committee," helping us hear the voice of God more clearly, and screening out interference or false messages.

Continual daily prayer may be the single most important practice for developing spiritual awareness. By pausing throughout the day to listen for the voice of God, we create an open channel through which God can clearly speak. Clare De Graaf has suggested the "10-Second Rule" for cultivating instant obedience to the voice of God: "Just do the next thing you're reasonably certain Jesus wants you to do. (And commit to it immediately—in the next ten seconds—before you change your mind!)"[2] This is a wonderful practice for cultivating receptivity to the voice of God. However, it works only if built on a foundation of the personal spiritual disciplines mentioned above and a pattern of responsiveness.

In what ways are you cultivating your capacity to hear what God is saying to you? Remember that it is possible to develop spiritual deafness, even if you once had a close relationship with the Lord. Each of us must be diligent in cultivating the personal practices that allow us to clearly discern the voice of God.

We Are Loved by God

A second evidence (and goal) of our surrender is that we may know that God loves us. This is no less important than being led by God. It could be argued that this evidence is even more important in that it is the foundation for our obedience. Follow Paul's thinking in Romans 8:14–15:

- Having surrendered to the Spirit, we are children of God (v. 14).
- We are freed from fear, enabled to live as true sons and daughters of God (v. 15).
- In fact, we have a close relationship to God and know him as our Father (v. 15).
- The inner witness of the Spirit communicates this relationship to us (v. 16).
- As children and heirs along with Christ, we are destined for glory (v. 17).

Our surrender to God results in a dramatic change in our status. We move from being foreigners, excluded from God's promises (Eph. 2:12) to being sons and daughters of God, heirs to all Christ's glory. And this same Spirit who guides our decision-making day by day also communicates to us that God deeply loves us, just as a father deeply loves his children.

Many Christians don't know this. While they may have an intellectual understanding that God loves all people and that they in particular are adopted into his family, they do not have a deep sense of being personally loved. One problem is that the resistance we have to surrendering to God at various points in our lives also forms a block in our relationship with the Spirit. When we do not allow ourselves to be led by the Spirit, we do not have the Spirit's witness of our close, loving relationship with the Father. We cultivate Spirit awareness as much to satisfy our own longing for love as to cultivate the obedience God requires. This is the substance of Paul's marvelous prayer for believers in Ephesians 3:14–19:

> For this reason I kneel before the Father, from whom
> every family in heaven and on earth derives its name.
> I pray that out of his glorious riches he may strengthen
> you with power through his Spirit in your inner being,
> so that Christ may dwell in your hearts through faith.
> And I pray that you, being rooted and established in
> love, may have power, together with all the Lord's holy
> people, to grasp how wide and long and high and
> deep is the love of Christ, and to know this love that
> surpasses knowledge—that you may be filled to the
> measure of all the fullness of God.

What a tremendous aspiration Paul had for all believers, that we may know how deeply we are loved! While many discussions of surrender focus on what we must do to be obedient to God, Paul's view of surrender was not subservience. We are not slaves to fear. Rather, we carry out the Father's will like loving children who are secure in his love and fully devoted to him. What we need, then, is not simply more self-discipline or more grudging obedience. That is surrender on the outside only. What we need is to increase our capacity to receive God's love. For when we do, our obedience will flow naturally from a satisfied soul. So how do we increase our capacity to receive the love of God?

The first and most obvious way is to surrender to God at the deepest possible level. The more we allow our surrender to float on the surface, surrendering in certain outward ways but allowing strongholds of resistance in our soul and spirit, the less we are able to receive God's love. When the Spirit cannot lead you, the Spirit cannot communicate God's love to you.

As you think about your own level of surrender in the three principal areas of spirit, soul, and body, how would you rate your level of surrender in each one? Are you 100 percent surrendered in body (that is, behavior) but only 50 percent surrendered in soul (mind and emotions)? Are you 25 percent surrendered in each area? As far as you are aware, are you fully surrendered to God in all areas? The more fully surrendered you are, the greater will be the Spirit-to-spirit connection within you, and the more you will understand and experience God's love for you.

Another way to increase your capacity to feel loved by God is to stop substituting or comparing your calling with that of others. It is tempting to compare our lives with others', trying to fulfill their calling rather than our own. We may try to live out another's conscience or giftedness or purpose because it is easier than doing the hard work of dealing with God at the level of the spirit, sorting out his call upon our own lives. That kind of life results in a creeping hollowness of soul, a deep dissatisfaction with ourselves and also with our relationship with God. It will not do to borrow someone else's conscience, copy someone else's gifts, or substitute someone else's purpose for the one God has given you. When you are willing to do the hard work of self-examination that results in accepting the gifts and calling God has given, your connection to the Spirit will be deeper and more active, and you will have a deeper and more powerful sense of God's love for *you*.

A third way to increase your capacity to receive God's love is to deal with the root causes of your behavior rather than settling for behavior modification. For example, you may rightly feel convicted about a problem such as anger in your life. Avoiding angry actions is the proper starting point for surrender. We surrender our impulse to experience angry outbursts, demeaning others through words, or even violence. But remember that behavior is always a symptom of a heart condition. On this subject, Paul wrote, "In your anger do not sin" (Eph. 4:26). Control your behavior, that's the first step. But you must deal with the deeper problem as well. "Do not let the sun go down while you are still angry, and do not give the devil a foothold" (vv. 26–27). It's not enough simply to avoid punching someone. You must address the relational issue, and do so quickly, then address the spirit-level problem so the Devil does not set up shop in your heart. To deepen your Spirit-to-spirit connection, allow God to work at the deepest levels of your heart.

Finally, to increase your awareness of God's love, shift your thinking from success to significance.[3] We Western Christians have a tendency to mark our lives, and even our relationships, in terms of achievement. We feel the best about our relationship with God when we are doing the most for God. This error rises naturally from our culture's focus on two things: outward appearance and success. The result in our lives is a spiritual shallowness that parallels our constant sense of material need. Although we are prosperous people, we always crave a little bit more achievement, money, and possessions. And, although God loves us and we are obedient to his will, we constantly believe we must do something more to merit his good favor.

The treatment for this condition is the same one I experienced in my offering plate moment of 2009, when I was forced to disassociate my sense of self from my position as the pastor of a thriving congregation. What I needed was to stand alone before God, to listen to his voice communicating to my spirit, telling me that I am loved and that my life has ultimate value regardless of my position.

To increase your capacity to receive the love of God, draw a distinction in your mind between who you *are* to God and what you *do* for him. Remember that the former is always more important than the latter. God loves you, not the things you do, the money you contribute, the hours you volunteer, or the good you do in the world. Those things are important, but not nearly as important as the Father's relationship with his precious child—you.

Live by the Spirit

Live by the Spirit. This simple idea, repeated so often in Paul's writing, is both the evidence and the goal of surrender. When we have abandoned ourselves fully to God, his Spirit is fully alive within us. We think differently. Our behavior changes. We have a new, stronger, and healthier sense of self. We become fully alive.

My prayer for you, and for all believers, is that you may choose "to grasp how wide and long and high and deep is the love of Christ, and to know this love that surpasses knowledge—that you may be filled to the measure of all the fullness of God" (Eph. 3:18–19). Surrender yourself to God. Open your heart and mind to him. Be transformed by his powerful love, and live your life to the fullest.

The Possibilities of Surrender

....

DO NOT BE
OVERCOME BY
EVIL, BUT OVERCOME
EVIL WITH GOOD.

ROMANS 12:21

Many Christians continue to see the concept of surrender and its parallel terms, *holiness* and *sanctification*, as a duty rather than an opportunity. Like prisoners who have become institutionalized, unable to accept the gift of freedom, we may prefer the smaller, more fearful, less satisfying life we can construct on our own to the fuller life we gain by surrendering to God. Yet there are consequences to not surrendering as the Spirit prompts us. We risk incurring negative results and missing the positive possibilities that surrender brings.

Each time the Spirit prompts the surrender of some area of life to him, we make a choice. We choose either to go deeper into surrender, giving up a little more of our body, soul, or spirit to the Lord, or to retrench, setting up greater resistance to the Spirit. The negative effects of our refusal to surrender are many. It may create doubt in our minds about our faith, about the goodness of God, or about our own salvation. Our refusal to surrender will certainly reduce our capacity to receive what God wants to give to us. We will miss out on freedom from sin or worry. We will miss out on opportunities to serve and to do so with joy. Refusal to surrender will precipitate double-mindedness (see James 1:8) that comes from a compartmentalized rather than completely consecrated life. Our refusal to surrender creates a block to the Spirit's work within us and our work for Christ in the world.

In contrast, when we choose to surrender, we are empowered to seize new possibilities. Paul closed his marvelous invitation to the surrendered life with this charge and encouragement: "Do not be overcome by evil, but overcome evil with good" (Rom. 12:21). We often hear this verse taught as a responsibility, and it is that. But it is also a possibility. We are challenged to do this because we are able to do so. As we walk by the Spirit, we really can reshape the world, overcoming the evil in our lives and communities with good. Surrender does not result in a passive, subservient existence. Instead, it frees and empowers us to be God's agents in the world.

Imagine the possibilities of surrender for your life. What might result in your personal life and relationships if you were able to fully devote yourself to God? How would it change your marriage, family relationships, or relationships with coworkers or fellow believers if you were fully self-aware, renewed in mind and spirit, appropriately humble, and empowered to do God's will? What would be the result in your community or nation if you were freed to live by the Spirit, freed from personal ambition, and empowered to enact God's vision?

As I discovered through my own offering plate moments, the instances when God calls us to a deeper level of surrender are uncomfortable and challenging. In each case, I faced the temptation to retreat into some aspect of self-protection or self-will. It would have been more comfortable for me to build houses than to accept God's call to build his kingdom. I first tried to cling to my safe and predictable vision for our family rather than to follow Jan's leading into the adventure of adopting a child. Perhaps no test of surrender was greater than my call to relinquish the safety and status of my position as a well-known senior pastor and follow the Spirit's leading to—what? I had no idea. In each case, I discovered that living in surrender is not merely challenging, but also best. While the offering plate may be uncomfortable at times, it is the best place to live.

Even Christ himself found this to be true. Scripture tells us that "during the days of Jesus' life on earth, he offered up prayers and petitions with fervent cries and tears to the one who could save him from death, and he was heard because of his reverent submission. Son though he was, he learned obedience from what he suffered and, once made perfect, he became the source of eternal salvation for all who obey him" (Heb. 5:7–9). Christ himself found the pathway to glory through submission. The same will be true for you and me. Our surrender is the doorway to a new and better life.

When will your next call to surrender come? What will be the context—your relationships? Ministry? Resources? Will it be a matter of body? Soul? Spirit? It is impossible to know. Perhaps you are facing some offering plate moment now, wondering if you have the faith to overcome your fear of surrender. I pray that you do find that faith. Whether you are now facing a moment of surrender, or whether that moment may come at some point in your future, I leave you with this simple prayer to guide you into a deeper experience of Christ's love. When you pray it with sincerity and conviction, you will discover a deeper experience of God than you have yet known.

> O merciful God, whatever you deny me, deny me not this love. Save me from the idolatry of "loving the world, or any of the things of the world." Let me never love any creature, but for your sake, and in subordination to your love. Take full possession of my heart; raise there your throne, and command there just as you do in heaven. Having been created by you, let me live for you; having been created for you, let me always act for your glory; having been redeemed by you, let me give to you what is yours, and let my spirit ever cleave to you alone.[1]

May God answer this prayer in your life in response to your willing surrender to the Spirit's call.

Notes

Chapter 4

1. Judson W. Van Deventner, "All to Jesus I Surrender," 1896, public domain.

Chapter 5

1. Gordon MacDonald, *Ordering Your Private World* (Nashville, TN: Thomas Nelson Publishers, 1984), 29–30.

2. Ibid., 58.

Chapter 7

1. "The Largest Churches 2015," Outreach.com, http://www.outreach magazine.com/outreach-100-largest-churches-2015.html?pag=2, and "The 100 Fastest-Growing Churches in America," Outreach.com, http://www.outreachmagazine.com/outreach-100-fastest-growing-churches-2015.html?pag=8.

Chapter 10

1. John and Charles Wesley, "List of Poetical Works," *The Works of John Wesley*, 3rd ed., vol. 14 (Kansas City, MO: Beacon Hill Press of Kansas City, 1979), 321.

2. Daniel Goleman, *Emotional Intelligence: Why It Can Matter More than IQ* (New York: Bantam Books, 1995).

3. Edwin H. Friedman, *A Failure of Nerve: Leadership in the Age of the Quick Fix* (New York: Seabury Books, 2007), 203.

Chapter 12

1. Richard A. Swenson, *Margin: Restoring Emotional, Physical, Financial, and Time Reserves to Overloaded Lives* (Colorado Springs, CO: NavPress, 2004), 195–196.

Chapter 14

1. James Weldon Johnson, "Dem Bones," https://en.wikipedia.org/wiki/Dem_Bones#The_song.

2. John Wesley, "An Extract of the Rev. Mr. John Wesley's Journal: From May 6, 1760 to October 28, 1972," *The Works of John Wesley*, 3rd ed., vol. 3 (Kansas City, MO: Beacon Hill Press of Kansas City, 1979), 144. Spelling modernized by the author.

Chapter 16

1. Marc Lawrence, *Two Weeks Notice,* written and directed by Marc Lawrence (Warner Home Video, 2002), DVD.

2. Clare De Graaf, *The 10-Second Rule: Following Jesus Made Simple* (New York: Howard Books, 2010), 15.

3. Many thanks to Lloyd Reeb for expounding on this distinction in his book *From Success to Significance: When the Pursuit of Success Isn't Enough* (Grand Rapids, MI: Zondervan, 2004), 14–15.

Chapter 17

1. Excerpt from "A Collection of Forms of Payer for Every Day in the Week" by John Wesley, *The Works of John Wesley,* vol. 11, 3rd ed. (Kansas City, MO: Beacon Hill Press of Kansas City, 1979), 205. Wording modernized by the author.